Rockhounding 101: Embark on a Thrilling Adventure.

Clinton .B Fellows

Rockhounding 101: Embark on a Thrilling Adventure. : Discover the Secrets of Rockhounding: A Beginner's Guide to Geological Exploration.

Funny helpful tips:

Maintain a culture of recognition; appreciating efforts boosts morale.

Seek mutual respect; it's the cornerstone of a healthy relationship.

<u>*Life advices:*</u>

Incorporate antioxidants into your diet; they combat free radicals and support overall health.

Every experience, good or bad, is a chapter in your life story; embrace each one as an opportunity for growth.

Introduction

This book is an extensive and invaluable guide for individuals passionate about exploring and collecting minerals. This comprehensive resource covers a wide range of topics related to mineral identification, rocks, mineral deposits, gemstones, maps, prospecting techniques, and protecting your finds. Whether you're a beginner or an experienced rockhound, this guide provides the essential knowledge and practical tips needed to enhance your rockhounding and prospecting adventures.

The guide begins with an introduction to minerals, offering an overview of their various properties and characteristics. It discusses the key aspects of mineral identification, including color, hardness, luster, cleavage, and crystal systems. With detailed explanations and helpful illustrations, readers will learn how to identify different minerals and gain a deeper understanding of their formation processes.

Moving on to rocks, the guide provides an introduction to the three main rock types: igneous, sedimentary, and metamorphic. It explores their origins, textures, and common examples, allowing readers to recognize and appreciate the diverse world of rocks. From the cooling of magma to the erosion and compaction of sediments, the guide explains the geological processes that contribute to the formation of each rock type.

The section on mineral deposits is particularly valuable for those interested in prospecting and mining. It delves into different types of deposits, starting with magmatic deposits formed from cooling magma. It then explores hydrothermal deposits, which result from mineral-rich fluids circulating through fractures in rocks. Secondary deposits, such as weathering and residual deposits, are also discussed, along with placer deposits formed by the mechanical action of water. The guide provides insights into the geological processes and conditions that lead to the formation of these deposits, as well as their economic significance.

Gemstones are another captivating aspect covered in the guide. It introduces readers to a wide range of precious and semi-precious gemstones, including diamonds, rubies, sapphires, emeralds, and many others. Readers will learn about the characteristics and properties that make each gemstone unique, as well as their geological occurrences and popular varieties. The guide also offers guidance on how to identify and evaluate gemstones, helping readers make informed decisions when building their collections or engaging in gemstone trading.

Prospecting techniques and the use of maps play a crucial role in successful rockhounding and prospecting endeavors. The guide provides practical tips on utilizing maps and geological data to identify potential collecting sites. It covers techniques such as panning, metal detecting, and rock sampling, equipping readers with the knowledge and skills needed to effectively search for minerals and precious stones.

In addition to the thrill of discovery, the guide emphasizes the importance of responsible collecting practices and protecting the environment. It highlights the significance of obtaining proper permits and mining claims, respecting private and public lands, and leaving the natural surroundings undisturbed. Readers will gain a deeper appreciation for the need to preserve natural resources and follow ethical guidelines in their rockhounding pursuits.

This book is a comprehensive reference that caters to the interests and needs of rockhounds and prospectors at various levels of experience. It combines scientific knowledge with practical advice, making it an indispensable companion for those passionate about rocks, minerals, and the thrill of discovery. Whether you're a hobbyist, a serious collector, or someone seeking to delve into the world of prospecting, this guide is an essential resource that will enhance your understanding and enjoyment of the fascinating world beneath our feet.

Contents

PART I — Mineral Identification

CHAPTER 1: Introduction to Minerals

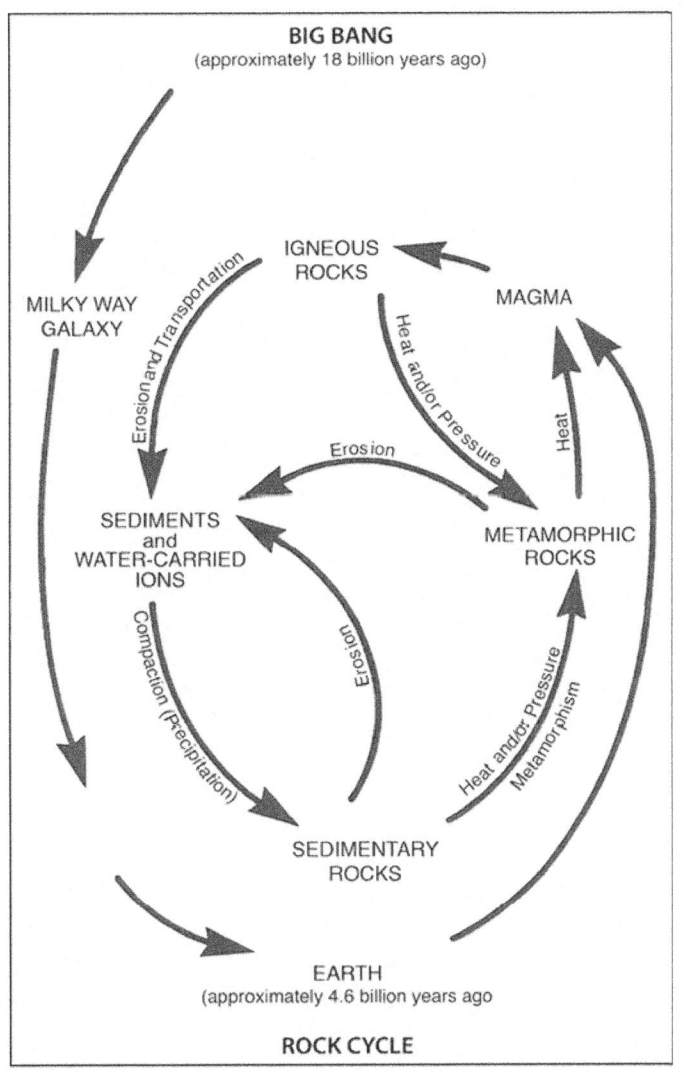

BIG BANG
(approximately 18 billion years ago)

MILKY WAY GALAXY

IGNEOUS ROCKS

MAGMA

Erosion and Transportation

Heat and/or Pressure

Heat

Erosion

SEDIMENTS and WATER-CARRIED IONS

METAMORPHIC ROCKS

Compaction (Precipitation)

Erosion

Heat and/or Pressure

Metamorphism

SEDIMENTARY ROCKS

EARTH
(approximately 4.6 billion years ago

ROCK CYCLE

THE EARTH

About 4.6 billion years ago the planets of our solar system began forming from a hot gaseous disc that surrounded the early sun. As the gas condensed solid mineral grains formed from which the planets accreted. Table 1-1 compares the order of relative abundances of the elements found in the universe, the sun, the earth, and the earth's crust.

TABLE 1-1
Order of Relative Abundances of the Elements
(by weight)

Universe	H	He	O	Ne	N	C	Si	Mg	Fe	S	A	Al	Ca	Na
Sun	H	He	O	Fe	Mg	N	Si	S	C	Ca	Al	Ni	Na	Cr
Whole Earth	Fe	O	Mg	Si	Ni	S	Ca	Al	Co	Na	Mn	K	Ti	P
Crust	O	Si	Al	Fe	Ca	Na	K	Mg	Ti	H	P	Mn	F	S
(Modified from Mason)														

During the accretion period the earth became a molten orb and there was stratification or zoning of material with the higher specific gravity (weight per unit volume) material concentrated in the core. Subsequent cooling resulted in the crystallization of minerals rich in oxygen and silicon, which formed the crustal rocks of the earth, much like slag forms during the process of iron smelting. A much simplified earth structure is listed in Table 1-2 and shown in Figure 1-1.

TABLE 1-2
Structure of the Earth

Name	Chemical Nature	Physical Nature	Specific Gravity
Atmosphere	N_2, O_2, H_2O, CO_2 inert gases	Gas	Less than 1
Hydrosphere (Oceans)	H_2O, salts	Liquid	1
Crust	Predominantly granites & basalts	Solid	2.5 - 3.0
Mantle	Mg, Fe silicates	Solid	3.0 - 8.0
Core	Fe - Ni alloy	Liquid - outer core Solid - inner core	10+

Our interest in rocks, minerals, and prospecting is in the crustal rocks of the Earth. Igneous and metamorphic rocks make up approximately 95 percent of the crustal rocks and sedimentary rocks make up the remaining five percent. However, sedimentary rocks cover approximately 75 percent of the land area.

The average elemental composition of the crust is listed in Table 1-3. Compare with Table 1-1.

FIGURE 1-1
Simplified Earth Cross-Section

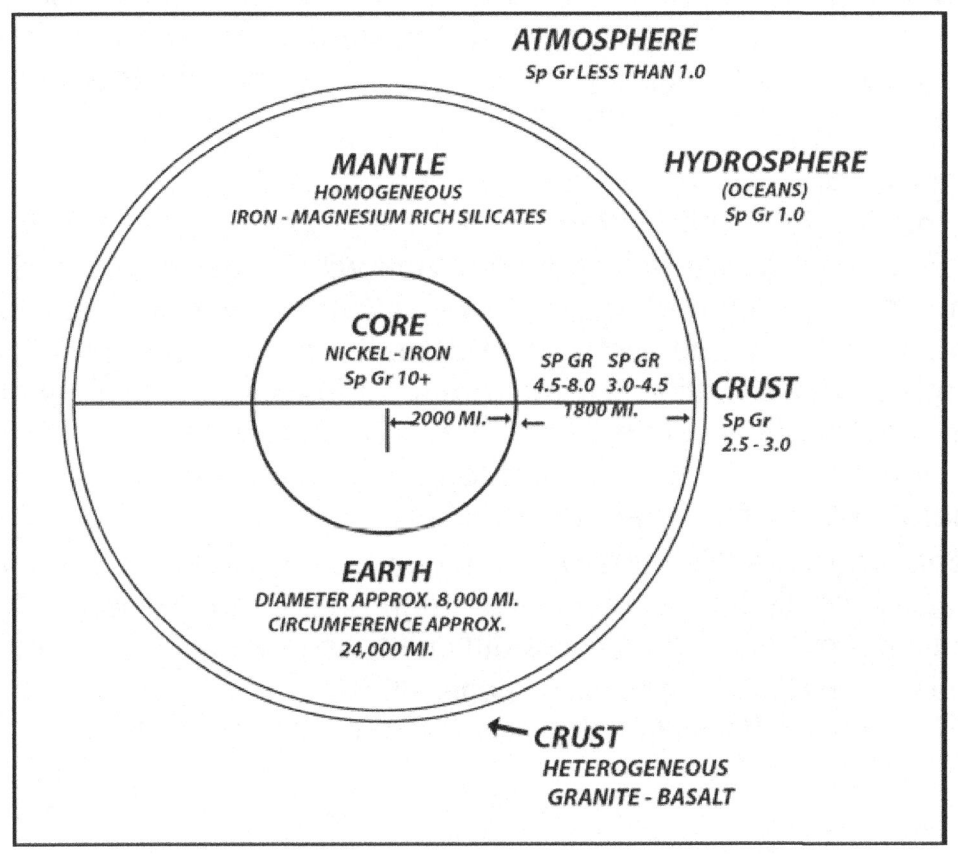

It should be noted that the base metals and rare and precious metals — copper, lead, zinc, gold, silver, etc. — fall within the "Remaining 75 Elements" category. This is why their occurrences are so rare. We are fortunate that, because of their economic value, their locations are usually delineated in mining districts and mine diggings throughout the country.

MINERALS

Approximately 3,000 different minerals have been identified, of which about 100 are fairly common and will be included in this book. A number of different mineral classifications are in use. Golden *Rocks and Minerals* and Simon and Schuster's *Rocks and Minerals* use a chemical classification of minerals. Minerals in this book are presented as they relate to the geologic environment in which they are found. This type of presentation aids in the study and understanding of mineral occurrences.

Learning to identify minerals is not difficult if you know what to look for and discipline yourself to memorize the mineral names. Identifying minerals is no more difficult than identifying people.

See Golden *Rocks and Minerals*, pages 66-69.

See Simon and Schuster's *Rocks and Minerals,* pages 51-55.

TABLE 1-3
Average Chemical Composition of the Crust

Element	Symbol	Wt. %	Vol. %
Oxygen	O	46.60	93.8
Silicon	Si	27.72	0.9
Aluminum	Al	8.13	0.5
Iron	Fe	5.00	0.4
Calcium	Ca	3.63	1.0
Sodium	Na	2.83	1.3
Potassium	K	2.59	1.8
Magnesium	Mg	2.09	0.3
Titanium	Ti		Tr
Hydrogen	H		Tr
Phosphorus	P		Tr
Manganese	Mn		Tr
Fluorine	F		Tr
Sulphur	S		Tr
Strontium	Sr		Tr
Barium	Ba		Tr
Carbon	C		Tr
Remaining 75 Elements		.037	
(Modified from Mason)		100%	100%

NOTE:
Symbols of chemical elements should be memorized.
See Simon and Schuster's *Rocks and Minerals*, page 54.
See Golden *Rocks and Minerals*, pages 271-273.

7

DEFINITION

A mineral is a homogeneous substance, composed of a specific chemical composition, and produced by natural inorganic processes.

See Golden *Rocks and Minerals,* page 5.

See Simon and Schuster's *Rocks and Minerals,* pages 8-9.

IDENTIFICATION OF MINERALS

Many minerals can be identified visually. Other minerals can be identified using very simple tests to determine their physical properties.

Chemical analysis is another means of mineral identification. Simple tests can be performed using a blowpipe. An excellent discussion of blowpipe analysis is found in *Prospecting and Mining* by Leo Mark Anthony. Other chemical tests are described in *Handbook for Small Mining Enterprises* by F.N. Earll, et al.

Optical properties of minerals can be observed with a microscope using mineral powder immersed in oil, or in thin sections. A thin section of rock is a thin wafer of the rock cut approximately I" by 2" with a diamond saw. The wafer is glued to a glass slide and then ground down using a polishing wheel until it is so thin that light will pass through it. A glass plate is then glued on top and the thin section can be viewed through a microscope. It is called a photomicrograph when photographed using polarized light.

See Simon and Schuster's *Rocks and Minerals,* Rx nos. 278, 284, 286 & 306.

Thin sections may be used as an accurate method to identify minerals and determine the percentage of minerals in a rock. Also, the shape and size of the grain may be studied to ascertain the origin and history of the rock. This is important to rock classification.

See Simon and Schuster's *Rocks and Minerals,* pages 427 (middle)-429.

X-ray analysis can be used to show the internal atomic properties of a mineral. This is a very accurate way to identify a mineral that cannot be identified by other methods.

See Golden *Rocks and Minerals,* page 59.
See Simon and Schuster's *Rocks and Minerals,* pages 47-51.

This book will be directed to teaching mineral identification using the "visual and simple testing of mineral properties" approach.

MINERAL PROPERTIES

The important first step in learning to identify minerals is learning mineral properties and how to test for them.

See Golden *Rocks and Minerals,* pages 52-58.
See Simon and Schuster's *Rocks and Minerals,* pages 38-46.
See *Prospecting for Gemstones and Minerals,* pages 34-37.

Supplies are few and relatively inexpensive. Most of the items listed below are necessary for the study of rocks and minerals and can be purchased at your local rock and gem shop: hand lens — lOX, pocket knife, magnet, acid bottle (dilute hydrochloric or nitric acid or muriatic acid in a small eyedropper bottle [CAUTION: use care in storing and carrying the acid bottle around]), streak plate (small piece of unglazed porcelain tile), and a hardness kit (optional). Also necessary are the following mineral specimens (several inches in size) to be used for testing properties: talc, gypsum, calcite, fluorite, feldspar, quartz, topaz, corundum, pyrite, chalcopyrite, hematite, galena, sphalerite, barite, magnetite, and halite.

All minerals are composed of atoms and, because the atoms and atomic structure vary, minerals have different properties. Many of the properties can be determined visually or by using simple tests. Become proficient at determining the following mineral properties:

1. COLOR — An obvious visual property. It is best to observe a fresh surface. Some colors are unique to certain minerals, such as malachite green, azurite blue, or rhodochrosite pink.

See Golden *Rocks and Minerals,* page 235.
See Simon and Schuster's *Rocks and Minerals,* mineral no. 92.

2. STREAK — The color of powder obtained by rubbing a mineral of hardness less than 5.5 to 6 on an unglazed porcelain plate (streak plate) can be diagnostic of a certain mineral, such as the reddish-brown streak of hematite.

See Golden *Rocks and Minerals,* page 57.

3. LUSTER — The sheen or gloss of a mineral's surface is determined by the way the light is reflected. The three main categories of luster are:

A. Metallic — looking like metal. Pyrite is an example.

See Simon and Schuster's *Rocks and Minerals,* mineral no. 31.

B. Nonmetallic — not looking like metal.

See Golden *Rocks and Minerals,* page 57.

C. Submetallic — between metallic and nonmetallic. Sphalerite is an example.

See Simon and Schuster's *Rocks and Minerals,* mineral no. 17.

4. HARDNESS — One of the most important tests used for identifying minerals is determining hardness. This test takes a little time to master, but it is absolutely necessary if you want to pursue minerals as a hobby. The German Mineralogist Freidrick Mohs (1773-1839) arranged 10 common minerals in order of increasing hardness and, since then, the hardness of all minerals has been rated according to his scale.

The Mohs Hardness Scale
1. Talc
2. Gypsum
 —fingernail (2.5)
3. Calcite
 —copper penny (3+)
4. Fluorite
5. Apatite
 —pocket knife, glass (5.5)
6. Orthoclase
7. Quartz
8. Topaz
9. Corundum
10. Diamond

See Golden *Rocks and Minerals,* page 55.
See Simon and Schuster's *Rocks and Minerals,* page 40.
See *Prospecting for Gemstones and Minerals,* page 35.

It should be pointed out that feldspar, Number 6 on the Hardness Scale in *Prospecting for Gemstones and Minerals*, is the name given to a group of minerals to which microcline and orthoclase belong. They all have a hardness of 6. Remember, minerals with a higher hardness number can scratch minerals with lower hardness numbers. Practice scratching the minerals recommended as supplies under the Mineral Properties Section until you get proficient. Obtaining a hardness kit is also useful.

5. CLEAVAGE AND FRACTURE — When minerals are struck with a hammer and broken, they will either break along definite planes or surfaces (cleavage), or they will break in an irregular or uneven manner (fracture).

See Golden *Rocks and Minerals,* pages 52-53.
See Simon and Schuster's *Rocks and Minerals,* page 39.

Cleavage can usually be identified as a flat surface from which light can be reflected if held in the right position. Cleavage can appear as a small step-like feature when the mineral is rotated to reflect the light. Minerals can have both cleavage and fracture on different sides. Do not confuse cleavage surfaces and crystal faces. Cleavage surfaces occur when the mineral is broken. Crystal faces are the outside surfaces of the mineral resulting from growth. When in doubt, break the mineral and observe the broken surface.

Examples of cleavage in three directions are galena and halite.
See Golden *Rocks and Minerals,* pages 91 & 121.

Examples of rhombohedral cleavage are calcite and dolomite.
See Golden *Rocks and Minerals,* pages 228-331.

Examples of cleavage in two directions are orthoclase and hornblende.

Examples of cleavage in one direction is the mica group of minerals.

See Simon and Schuster's *Rocks and Minerals,* mineral nos. 225, 229, and 230.

Examples of conchoidal fracture are quartz and chert.

See Golden *Rocks and Minerals,* pages 207-209.

Note that quartz and chert have no cleavage, only conchoidal fracture. Quartz crystals are one of the best examples to see crystal faces which can be compared with cleavage surfaces.

6. SPECIFIC GRAVITY — Specific gravity or "heft" of a mineral is its weight per unit volume or, simply put, how heavy a mineral feels when held in the hand. Specific gravity can aid in identification of some minerals and, with a little practice, one can learn to estimate specific gravity just by holding the mineral and classifying it as light, medium or average, heavy or very heavy.

Mineral	Specific Gravity	Class
Halite	2.1 gm/cm^3	Light
Gypsum	2.3	Light
Quartz	2.7	Avg. or Med.
Barite	4.5	Heavy
Galena	7.6	Very Heavy
Gold	19.3	Super Heavy

7. MAGNETISM — Three minerals we will study attract a magnet. Magnetite has a strong magnetic attraction. Pyrrhotite and ilmenite are weakly attracted. The best type of magnet is a "stud finder," which is quite sensitive.

8. TASTE — Halite tastes salty and sylvite has a bitter taste.

9. ACID TEST — Several carbonate minerals react with acid. Calcite shows a strong effervescent reaction to acid (dilute hydrochloric, nitric acid or muriatic acid). Dolomite shows a weaker reaction. Be sure to wash the mineral after using acid. Also, use care not to get acid on anything but the mineral — one drop will do — and quickly wash anything coming in contact with the acid.

Practice determining the above nine mineral properties until you become proficient.

Below is a form which can be used:

Properties	
Color:	Cleavage:
Streak:	Fracture:
Luster:	Specific Gravity:
Hardness:	Other:

MINERAL IDENTIFICATION DETERMINATIVE TABLES

Included in the Appendix of this book are determinative tables that can be used as an aid in mineral identification. The tables are organized using mineral properties of luster, hardness, and cleavage. The major classification is that of metallic and nonmetallic luster. Secondary classification is based on mineral hardness.

The determinative tables can be a real aid in mineral identification. Get in the habit of using the tables once you have recorded the properties.

ATOMIC STRUCTURE OF MINERALS

All minerals are composed of atoms, which combine to form molecules and bind together chemically in different ways to give minerals their characteristic properties. Basic atomic theory, though not absolutely necessary for the study of rocks and minerals, is interesting in that it explains certain observable features in minerals, such as fracture and cleavage.

See Golden *Rocks and Minerals,* pages 18-35.

See Simon and Schuster's *Rocks and Minerals,* pages 22 (bottom)-27.

CRYSTALS

Most all minerals can occur in crystal form if the proper environment existed for crystal growth at the time of formation. There are seven crystal systems.

Isometric (cubic) System

Hexagonal System

Trigonal (Rhombohedral) System

Tetragonal System

Orthorhombic System

Monoclinic System

Triclinic System

Recognizing mineral crystals is an aid to mineral identification.

See Golden *Rocks and Minerals,* pages 38-51.

See Simon and Schuster's *Rocks and Minerals,* pages 9-22 and 27-37.

However, note that six crystal systems are listed in Simon and Schuster's *Rocks and Minerals*, page 15. Simon and Schuster is incorrect in listing Rhombohedral as a subdivision of the Hexagonal System. It is recognized as a separate crystal system.

Crystallography can be a difficult subject to fully understand. Unless you are seriously interested in crystallography, just skim the material.

PART II — Rocks
CHAPTER 2: Introduction to Rocks

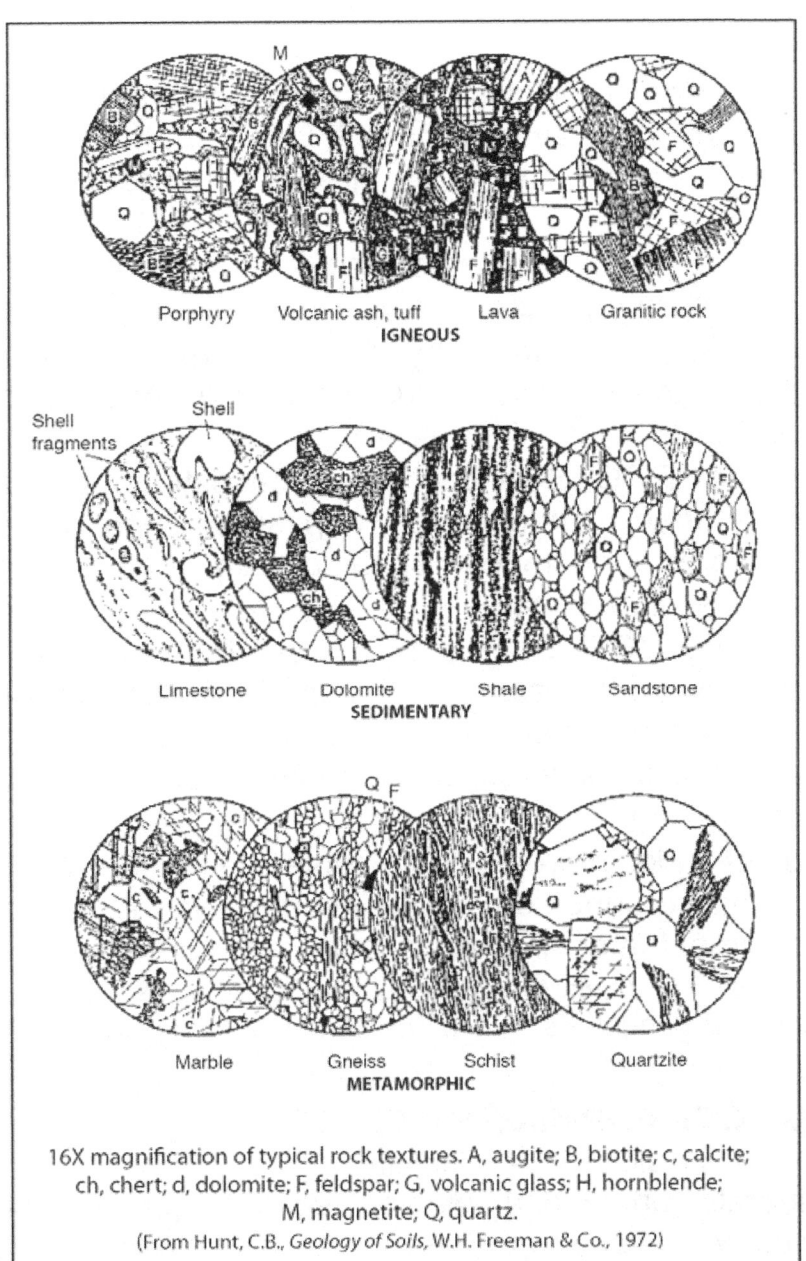

IGNEOUS

Porphyry · Volcanic ash, tuff · Lava · Granitic rock

SEDIMENTARY

Limestone · Dolomite · Shale · Sandstone

Shell fragments · Shell

METAMORPHIC

Marble · Gneiss · Schist · Quartzite

16X magnification of typical rock textures. A, augite; B, biotite; c, calcite; ch, chert; d, dolomite; F, feldspar; G, volcanic glass; H, hornblende; M, magnetite; Q, quartz.
(From Hunt, C.B., *Geology of Soils,* W.H. Freeman & Co., 1972)

ROCK TYPES

A basic knowledge of rocks is necessary to understand minerals and their occurrences. However, to benefit fully from the investment that goes into prospecting, an even greater knowledge of rocks is necessary.

Rocks are natural aggregates of one or more minerals and can be classified into three main groups:

IGNEOUS ROCKS — form by the cooling of molten material beneath the earth's surface (intrusive), and on or near the surface related to volcanic activity (extrusive).

SEDIMENTARY ROCKS — form from pre-existing rock material that has been eroded, transported, deposited, and cemented or solidified, such as sandstone or shale, or from chemical precipitation in water, such as limestone.

METAMORPHIC ROCKS — form from pre-existing rocks that have been recrystallized because of changes in temperature and/or pressure caused by deep burial and crustal movement (regional metamorphic rocks) or intrusion by molten igneous rocks (contact metamorphic rocks).

The study of rocks, petrology, is a subject in itself and this book will provide a background of basic information necessary for an understanding of the environments of mineral formation.

See *Prospecting for Gemstones and Minerals,* pages 79-86.

See Simon and Schuster's *Rocks and Minerals,* pages 55, 58-59, and 414-415.

IGNEOUS ROCK FORMING MINERALS

* Minerals you should be able to identify.

Three minerals, orthoclase, plagioclase and quartz, make up the bulk of nearly all igneous rocks. Thirteen additional minerals — adularia, microcline, sanidine, perthite, cristobalite, olivine, nepheline, sodalite, leucite, biotite, hornblende, pyroxene, and muscovite — are also found in igneous rocks in percentages of approximately 1 to 10 percent. Their occurrence is controlled by the chemical environment of crystallization.

It is interesting to compare the chemical formulas of these rock forming minerals with Table 1-3 showing Average Chemical Composition of the Crust. You will notice that the eight elements O, Si, Al, Fe, Ca, Na, K and Mg are among the elements found making up the igneous rock minerals.

See Golden *Rocks and Minerals,* pages 214-221.

See Simon and Schuster's *Rocks and Minerals,* mineral nos. 253-259.

See Prospecting for *Gemstones and Minerals,* page 87 (chemical composition).

FELDSPAR is a group name given to the following minerals: orthoclase, adularia, microcline, sanidine, perthite and plagioclase.

ORTHOCLASE* — $KAlSi_3O_8$. Pink to white in color, hardness 6, good cleavage.

See Simon and Schuster's *Rocks and Minerals,* Rx no. 280 (3rd photograph) — slightly pinkish large orthoclase crystals in the photograph of porphyritic tonalite.

See Simon and Schuster's *Rocks and Minerals,* Rx no. 278 — pink orthoclase in the red granite photograph.

See Simon and Schuster's *Rocks and Minerals,* Rx no. 278 (one page after red granite) —white orthoclase in the white granite photograph.

See Simon and Schuster's *Rocks and Minerals,* mineral no. 254.

See Golden *Rocks and Minerals,* page 216.

Orthoclase commonly occurs as a twinned crystal in igneous rocks.

See Golden *Rocks and Minerals,* page 217 (center).

This Carlsbad twinning shows up by reflecting the crystal surface in the light. You will see the two different reflections approximately dividing the crystal in half.

See Simon and Schuster's *Rocks and Minerals,* Rx no. 281 — see the photomicrograph (thin section) at bottom of page. Note the upper lefthand corner of photomicrograph for twinned orthoclase crystal.

See Simon and Schuster's *Rocks and Minerals,* Rx no. 307 — see the photomicrograph of thin section at bottom of page. Note the large twinned orthoclase crystal in the right half of the photomicrograph.

See Simon and Schuster's *Rocks and Minerals,* Rx no. 300 — see the orthoclase crystal without twinning in the upper righthand corner of the photomicrograph of thin section at the bottom of the page.

ADULARIA — $KAlSi_3O_8$. A low temperature equivalent to orthoclase.

See Golden *Rocks and Minerals,* page 216.

See Simon and Schuster's *Rocks and Minerals,* mineral no. 256.

MICROCLINE — $KAlSi_3O_8$. Feldspar, commonly greenish-blue, found in pegmatites or metamorphic rocks.

See Golden *Rocks and Minerals,* page 214.

See Simon and Schuster's *Rocks and Minerals,* mineral no. 255.

SANIDINE — $KAlSi_3O_8$. High temperature feldspar found in volcanics.

See Golden *Rocks and Minerals,* page 214.

See Simon and Schuster's *Rocks and Minerals,* mineral no. 253.

PERTHITE — An intergrowth of minerals, microcline and the plagioclase mineral, anorthite.

See Golden *Rocks and Minerals,* page 216.

See Simon and Schuster's *Rocks and Minerals,* mineral no. 257.

PLAGIOCLASE* — $(Na,Ca) AlSi_2O_8$. A group of six minerals (albite, oligoclase, andesine, labradorite, bytownite and anorthite) formed from solid solution.

See Simon and Schuster's *Rocks and Minerals,* mineral nos. 258, 259.

See Golden *Rocks and Minerals,* pages 218-221.

White to gray in color, hardness 6, good cleavage. Appears as white tabular crystals in igneous rocks, but not necessarily distinct.

See Simon and Schuster's *Rocks and Minerals,* Rx no. 318 — tabular plagioclase crystals in diorite rock sample.

See Simon and Schuster's *Rocks and Minerals,* Rx. nos. 280 and 286 — the white minerals in these rock samples of tonalite and olivine gabbro are plagioclase.

As can be seen, plagioclase minerals are rather nondescript, and when they occur in the same rock with white orthoclase, can be difficult to differentiate with the naked eye or hand lens.

Plagioclase minerals also twin, but in a different form than orthoclase. The twinning occurs as lamellae or striations, rarely visible to the naked eye or hand lens. An example of plagioclase twinning is shown below.

See Golden *Rocks and Minerals,* page 219 (at center), and page 221 (at bottom right).

The twinning lamellae or striations show up quite well in thin sections.

See Simon and Schuster's *Rocks and Minerals,* Rx no. 284 — see far left center of photomicrograph of thin section of diorite.

See Simon and Schuster's *Rocks and Minerals,* Rx no. 286 — see scattered striated plagioclase crystals in photomicrograph of thin section of olivine gabbro.

QUARTZ* — SiO_2. Many igneous rocks contain the mineral quartz, typically as gray to glassy blebs. Hardness 7, conchoidal fracture.

See Golden *Rocks and Minerals,* pages 206-207.

See Simon and Schuster's *Rocks and Minerals,* Rx no. 278 — rock specimen of red granite. Note the small gray, glassy blebs scattered throughout the orthoclase.

The minerals listed below — olivine, nepheline, sodalite and leucite — can occur in some igneous rocks where there is a deficiency of silica.

OLIVINE* — $(Mg,Fe)_2SiO_4$. A solid solution group of minerals sometimes found in igneous rocks, but never with quartz; commonly found as small blebs in basalt. Light "apple green" in color, hardness 6.5-7, conchoidal fracture.

See Golden *Rocks and Minerals,* pages 164-165.
See Simon and Schuster's *Rocks and Minerals,* mineral no. 159.

Nepheline, sodalite and leucite are called feldspathoids and have similar composition to the feldspar minerals, but contain less silica.

NEPHELINE — $Na_3KAl_4Si_4O_{16}$. Quite rare in the western United States. Can be confused with plagioclase. Does not occur with quartz. White to gray in color, hardness 5.6-6, poor cleavage, greasy luster is diagnostic. Plagioclase does not have a greasy luster.

See Golden *Rocks and Minerals,* pages 222-223.
See Simon and Schuster's *Rocks and Minerals,* mineral no. 249 and Rx no. 289.

SODALITE — $Na_8(Al_6Si_6O_{24})C_{12}$. Distinctive blue color, not found with quartz.

See Golden *Rocks and Minerals,* page 224.
See Simon and Schuster's *Rocks and Minerals,* mineral no. 262.

LEUCITE — $KAlSi_2O_6$. Relatively rare, not found with quartz. Usually occurs in separate scattered crystals. White to gray in color, hardness 5.5-6, conchoidal fracture.

See Golden *Rocks and Minerals,* pages 224-225.
See Simon and Schuster's *Rocks and Minerals,* mineral no. 252 and Rx nos. 308, 309 and 311.

The following three minerals — biotite, hornblende and pyroxene occur as disseminated black minerals and make up 1 to 10 percent of most igneous rocks. They can occur as the only black mineral seen, or in combinations of two, but rarely all three together and can be very difficult to tell apart.

See Simon and Schuster's *Rocks and Minerals,* Rx nos. 278 and 279.

BIOTITE* — $K(FeMg)_2(Si_3)O_{10}(OH)_2$. Black mica. Forms in small thin "books" and can be peeled in thin sheets. Black in color with vitreous luster, hardness 2.5-3, perfect cleavage.

See Golden *Rocks and Minerals,* pages 194-195.

See Simon and Schuster's *Rocks and Minerals,* mineral no. 230.

HORNBLENDE* — $(Ca,Na,K)_2(MgFeAl)_5(SiAl)_8O_{22}(OH,F)_2$.

Complex silicate. Black in color, often with a greenish tinge, hardness 5-6, cleavage in two directions. Tabular mineral which can be very difficult to tell from pyroxene. Can be identified by crystal cross section which can sometimes be seen in the rock.

See Golden *Rocks and Minerals,* pages 184-185.

See Simon and Schuster's *Rocks and Minerals,* Rx nos. 280 and 292.

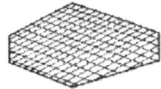

Hornblende crystal cross section

PYROXENE — $(Ca,Mg,Fe,Ti,Al)_2(Si,Al)_2O_6$. A group name for a number of minerals, the most common of which are augite, enstatite, hypersthene, hedenbergite and diopside. Black with a greenish tinge to green in color, hardness of 5-5.6, cleavage in two directions. Augite and hypersthene are very difficult to tell from hornblende. The crystal cross-section differs from that of hornblende.

See Golden *Rocks and Minerals,* pages 174-179.

Pyroxene crystal cross section

MUSCOVITE* — $KAl_2(Si_3Al)O_{10}(OH)_2$ — White mica. Found in some granites and pegmatites. Colorless to various light shades of color, hardness 2.5-3, perfect cleavage — peels apart in thin sheets.

See Golden *Rocks and Minerals,* pages 194-195.

See Simon and Schuster's *Rocks and Minerals,* mineral no. 225 (note associated milky quartz) and Rx no. 320.
See *Prospecting for Gemstones and Minerals,* pages 87-89.

CHAPTER 3: Igneous Rocks

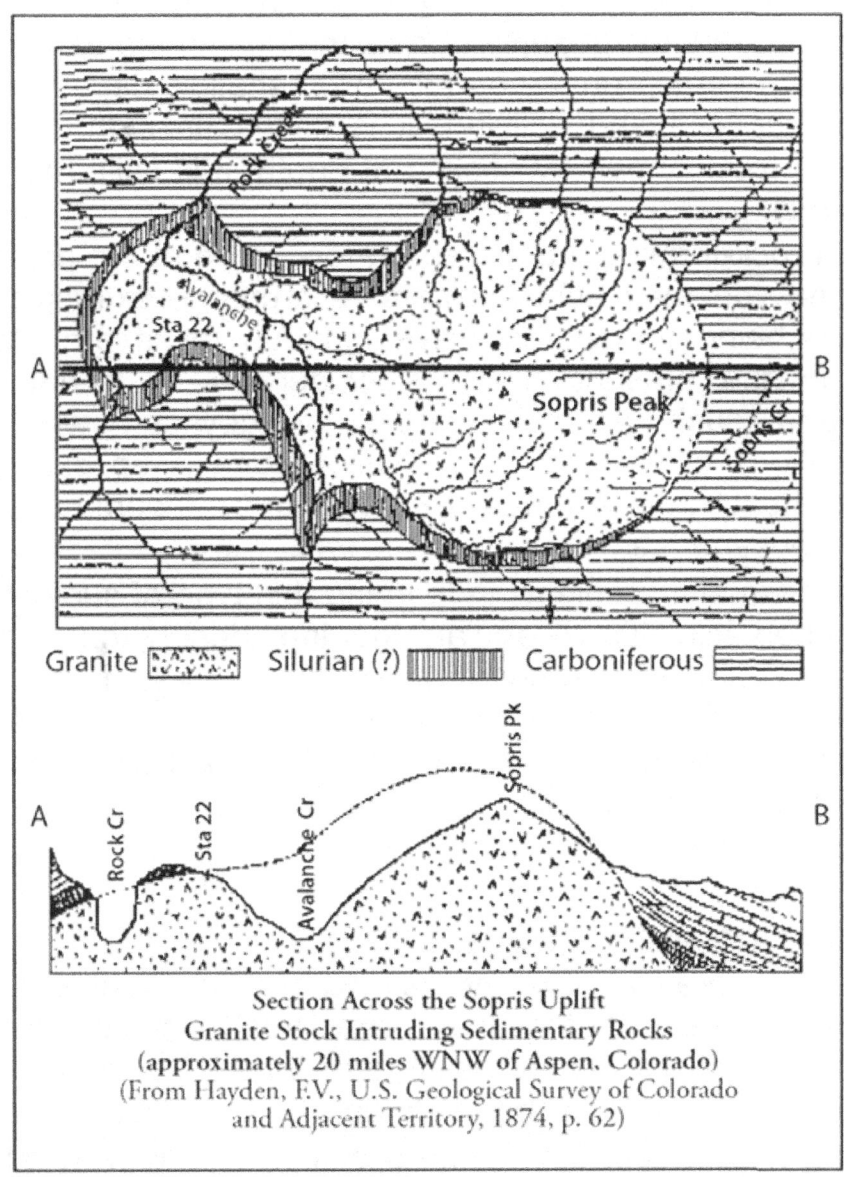

Granite · Silurian (?) · Carboniferous

Section Across the Sopris Uplift
Granite Stock Intruding Sedimentary Rocks
(approximately 20 miles WNW of Aspen, Colorado)
(From Hayden, F.V., U.S. Geological Survey of Colorado
and Adjacent Territory, 1874, p. 62)

INTRODUCTION

Igneous rocks form by the cooling of magma (molten material) and make up the greatest quantity of rock material in the earth's crust. If the rock was formed on the surface or at shallow depths (related to volcanic eruptions and activity), it is called an extrusive igneous rock. If the rock formed by cooling at depth, it is called an intrusive igneous rock.

Igneous rock-forming processes are occurring at the present time. Every time you read about volcanoes erupting, extrusive igneous rocks are being formed. Intrusive igneous rocks are also being formed at the present time, as evidenced by certain surface phenomena such as hot springs or geysers, which reflect concentrations of heat at depth. Yellowstone is an example. The source of heat in these areas is thought to be magma at depths of several thousand feet.

One of the major problems in learning this type of subject material is the related scientific vocabulary that is suddenly thrust upon you. There is no easy way around it. If you are interested enough, learn the meanings of the new words, even though it can be frustrating at times. It will be worth it in the long run. A glossary of terms can be found on page 105, herein.

See Golden *Rocks and Minerals,* pages 6-8.
See *Prospecting for Gemstones and Minerals,* pages 86-87.

CLASSIFICATION OF IGNEOUS ROCKS

Igneous rocks are classified by their mineral composition and mode of occurrence, i.e., whether they are extrusive or intrusive. I have prepared an Igneous Rock Classification Chart, Table 3-1. Compare it with the oversimplified chart in Golden *Rocks and Minerals*, page 9.

At first glance Table 3-1 appears complex; however, after going over it and understanding it, you will find that it makes sense and, more importantly, it works. You should memorize the chart.

The first vertical column on the left side of the chart classifies by depth of formation, working from surface (extrusive) rocks down to deeper and deeper formed (intrusive) rocks.

TABLE 3-1
Igneous Rock Chart

DEPTH OF OCCURRENCE	TEXTURE	LIGHT COLOR — SILICIC (75-66%) 100-66% ORTHOCLASE / 0-33% PLAGIOCLASE		DARK COLOR — INTERMEDIATE (66-52%) 66-33% ORTHOCLASE / 33-66% PLAGIOCLASE				VERY DARK COLOR — MAFIC (52-45%) 33-0% ORTHOCLASE / 66-100% PLAGIOCLASE		BLACK — ULTRAMAFIC (45-40%) NO FELDSPARS	
ACCESSORY MINERALS		NO QUARTZ (NEPHELINE) HORNBLENDE BIOTITE	QUARTZ BIOTITE HORNBLENDE PYROXENE	NO QUARTZ BIOTITE HORNBLENDE PYROXENE	QUARTZ BIOTITE HORNBLENDE PYROXENE	NO QUARTZ BIOTITE HORNBLENDE PYROXENE	QUARTZ BIOTITE HORNBLENDE PYROXENE	NO OLIVINE BIOTITE HORNBLENDE PYROXENE	OLIVINE PYROXENE HORNBLENDE	NO OLIVINE PYROXENE HORNBLENDE	OLIVINE PYROXENE HORNBLENDE
EXTRUSIVE ROCKS — SURFACE LAVA FLOWS	GLASS FRAGMENTAL	OBSIDIAN, PERLITE, PUMICE, ASH, AGGLOMERATE, BRECCIA									
EXTRUSIVE ROCKS — SURFACE FLOWS, DIKES & SILLS	APHANITIC (CAN'T BE SEEN) / FINE-GRAINED PORPHYRITIC	TRACHYTE (PHONOLITE)	RHYOLITE	LATITE	QUARTZ LATITE	ANDESITE	DACITE	BASALT	OLIVINE BASALT		
		FELSITE (LIGHT COLOR)						TRAP (DARK COLOR)			
INTRUSIVE ROCKS — ASSOCIATED WITH DEEP INTRUSIVES AS DIKES AND SILLS	FINE-GRAINED (SUGARY)		APLITE								
	VERY COARSE-GRAINED		PEGMATITE								
INTRUSIVE ROCKS — SHALLOW TO DEEP INTRUSIVES, STOCK <40 SQ. MILES, BATHOLITH >40 SQ. MILES, SURFACE EXPOSURE	MEDIUM TO COARSE GRAINED PORPHYRITIC	SYENITE	GRANITE	MONZONITE	QUARTZ MONZONITE	DIORITE	QUARTZ DIORITE OR GRANO DIORITE	GABBRO, DIABASE, NORITE, ANORTHOSITE	OLIVINE GABBRO	PYROXENITE HORNBLENDITE	PERIDOTITE (KIMBERLITE) DUNITE

NOTE: RE BASALTS: IF <50% VESICLES IT IS CALLED VESICULAR BASALT. IF >50% VESICLES IT IS CALLED SCORIA

28

Crystal size is often an indication of depth of cooling. A general rule of thumb is that rocks that cool on the surface, such as lavas, or near the surface have crystals too small to see with the eye or extremely small crystals, simply because they cooled so rapidly the crystals just didn't have time to grow.

See Simon and Schuster's *Rocks and Minerals,* Rx no. 306—Basalt.

Extremely rapid cooling, such as when a lava flow makes contact with the air, water of a river, lake or ocean may result in the formation of volcanic glass.

See Simon and Schuster's *Rocks and Minerals,* Rx no. 314.

In general, the more slowly an igneous rock cools, the larger its crystals should grow. Commonly, crystals may be growing at depth in a magma (molten mass) and because of some crustal disturbance the magma will begin to work its way toward the surface, resulting in volcanic activity. The crystals that had already formed at depth can end up embedded in a fine-grained lava rock. The term porphyritic refers to these larger crystals found in a groundmass of fine crystals. If the larger crystals make up more than 50% of the rock, the rock is called a PORPHYRY.

See Simon and Schuster's *Rocks and Minerals,* Rx nos. 280 (bottom of second page) and 318.

With undisturbed cooling at depth for a long period of time, the rock will show a well-developed medium to coarse grained texture.

See Simon and Schuster's *Rocks and Minerals,* Rx no. 280 (bottom of second page).

At rare times the condition of cooling and chemical composition at depth might be right for the formation of rocks with a fine sugary grain texture (APLITE) or with very large crystals, in some cases several feet in size (PEGMATITE).

It should be remembered that we have been talking in generalities, and that in reality numerous varieties of conditions of cooling can exist along with numerous varieties of chemical compositions, so that there are always exceptions to what you expect to observe.

The top horizontal part of the Igneous Rock Chart contains the essential and accessory minerals used for classifying igneous rocks. Looking first at the feldspars in the rock, it is necessary to determine how much of the feldspar is orthoclase and how much is plagioclase. This will allow you to select vertical columns to follow down. Also note that on the far right side of the chart is a column where rocks contain no feldspars.

Secondly, after determining the percentages of orthoclase and plagioclase, it must be determined whether or not the rock contains quartz. This will give the proper sub-column to follow down.

Discussion of visual identification of percentages of orthoclase, plagioclase and quartz in igneous rocks is great in theory but in reality it may be difficult or impossible to visually identify these minerals because the orthoclase and plagioclase can be very similar in appearance, or the rock may be too fine grained to see the orthoclase, plagioclase or quartz. The only accurate way to classify igneous rock may be by making a thin section of it. See discussion of thin sections in this book. With a thin section of the rock, orthoclase, plagioclase and quartz may be seen through a microscope and can easily be identified.

See Simon and Schuster's *Rocks and Minerals* (photomicrographs), Rx nos. 278, 284, 286, 300 and 306.

There are some "tricks of the trade" or general rules of thumb I can give you so you may make "educated" guesses in naming igneous rocks.

Notice the top of the Rock Chart listing color as light, intermediate, dark or very dark. Light colored (silicic) rocks generally fall in the region containing 100% to 66% of orthoclase of the feldspar content in columns on the left side of the chart.

See Simon and Schuster's *Rocks and Minerals,* Rx nos. 278 (three rock samples), 281, 282, 300 and 304. Note Rx no. 280 (second and third rock samples) are somewhat darker because of a greater percentage of black minerals.

Intermediate colored rocks generally fall in the column containing nearly equal percentages of orthoclase and plagioclase to predominantly plagioclase found in the central columns of the chart.

See Simon and Schuster's *Rocks and Minerals,* Rx nos. 283, 284, 302 and 305.

Dark colored (mafic or ultramafic) rocks generally contain plagioclase as the predominant feldspar, and those rocks in the far right columns have little or no feldspars.

See Simon and Schuster's *Rocks and Minerals,* Rx nos. 286, 287, 288, 290, 291, 292, 293, 294, 295, 296 and 306.

EXTRUSIVE IGNEOUS ROCKS

Volcanic activity produces an interesting variety of rocks. During initial stages of the evolution of a volcano, a vent must be cleared before lava flows can occur. Fragmental rock is propelled into the air by gas pressure and falls back around the vent as cinder material, forming a cinder cone. The cinder material, if later consolidated, forms a rock called volcanic AGGLOMERATE. Finer material ejected into the air can travel substantial distances in the wind as volcanic ash. Volcanic ash settles back to earth on land or in lakes, streams or oceans, sometimes over thousands of square miles, inches to feet deep. The Mount St. Helens eruption of 1980 is a perfect example. Unconsolidated, it remains volcanic ash, which usually appears light gray in color with traces of stratification. If later consolidated, usually in water, the rock called TUFF is formed. Tuff is a buff-colored sedimentary rock, and will be discussed in the sedimentary rock section of this book.

Once a throat is cleared, lava flows can commence. Chemical composition and quantity of gas mixed with the lava will affect how fluid the lava will flow. Mafic lavas are generally more fluid, flowing easier than silicic lavas. Gas mixed with lava at the time of eruption is evidenced by vesicles in the cooled lava.

Under certain special conditions, a hot gas cloud consisting of ash, crystals and cinders may occur during an eruption, and when it settles and cools forms a rock called IGNIMBRITE (welded tuff), generally rhyolitic in composition.

See Simon and Schuster's *Rocks and Minerals,* Rx no. 349.

Lava, rapidly cooled in water or air, forms as volcanic glass called OBSIDIAN, or VITROPHYRE, if it contains plagioclase crystals in a glass groundmass.

See Simon and Schuster's *Rocks and Minerals,* Rx no. 314.

Obsidian weathers (devitrifies) easily forming PERLITE.

See *Prospecting for Gemstones and Minerals,* page 89.

Because of the water content in perlite, it can be crushed and heated in a kiln, popping like popcorn, and giving it special qualities as a lightweight aggregate.

Lava ejected with much gas will cool as a frothy rock called PUMICE, which has a specific gravity of less than 1, so it will float on water.

See Simon and Schuster's *Rocks and Minerals,* Rx no. 315.

Lava flows cool forming volcanic rocks that can vary in mineral composition. The various rock types are listed in the bottom horizontal row in the extrusive rock section of the Igneous Rock Chart from left to right.

TRACHYTE — See Simon and Schuster's *Rocks and Minerals,* Rx no. 304.

RHYOLITE — See Simon and Schuster's *Rocks and Minerals,* Rx no. 299 and 300.

LATITE — See Simon and Schuster's *Rocks and Minerals,* Rx no. 303.

QUARTZ LATITE

ANDESITE — See Simon and Schuster's *Rocks and Minerals,* Rx no. 305.

DACITE — See Simon and Schuster's *Rocks and Minerals,* Rx no. 302.

BASALT — See Simon and Schuster's *Rocks and Minerals,* Rx no. 306.

Gas vesicles, if they occur, are generally found in basalts. If the vesicles make up less than 50 percent of the volume of the rock, it is called vesicular basalt. If the vesicles make up more than 50 percent of the volume of the rock, it is called SCORIA.

FELSITE is the name given to silicic or intermediate very fine-grained volcanic rock which has cooled very rapidly. Since the grains cannot be seen with the naked eye, its texture is termed aphanitic.

Because of all the variables in composition and eruption, volcanic rocks vary in color from place to place. For example, rhyolites can be off-white, gray, buff, light brown, or light purple.

See *Prospecting for Gemstones and Minerals,* pages 89-100 (top).

INTRUSIVE IGNEOUS ROCKS

Most intrusive igneous rocks in the western United States formed some 40 to 100 million years ago. Cooling, often several thousand feet below the surface, they are now exposed because of erosion, over tens or hundreds of square miles. A surface exposure of "granitic" type rock of greater than 40 square miles is called a BATHOLITH. If less than 40 square miles, the rock exposed is called a STOCK.

The Sierra Nevada batholith and the Idaho batholith are two well-known batholiths in the western United States.

See Simon and Schuster's *Rocks and Minerals,* pages 415-419 (the igneous process).

As with extrusive rocks, intrusive rocks are classified and named depending upon orthoclase and plagioclase percentage of the feldspar and quartz content. On the bottom row of Table 3-1 starting on the left side, we have:

SYENITE — See Simon and Schuster's *Rocks and Minerals,* Rx no. 281, 282 and 289.

APLITE — See Simon and Schuster's *Rocks and Minerals,* Rx no. 321 and page 415.

PEGMATITE — See Simon and Schuster's *Rocks and Minerals,* Rx no. 320.

GRANITE — See Simon and Schuster's *Rocks and Minerals,* Rx no. 277, 278 and 316.

MONZONITE — See Simon and Schuster's *Rocks and Minerals,* Rx no. 283.

QUARTZ MONZONITE

DIORITE — See Simon and Schuster's *Rocks and Minerals,* Rx no. 284 and 318.

TONALITE — See Simon and Schuster's *Rocks and Minerals,* Rx no. 280.

QUARTZ DIORITE or GRANODIORITE — See Simon and Schuster's *Rocks and Minerals,* Rx no. 279.

GABBRO — See Simon and Schuster's *Rocks and Minerals,* Rx no. 285 and 286.

DIABASE — See Simon and Schuster's *Rocks and Minerals,* Rx no. 319.

NORITE — See Simon and Schuster's *Rocks and Minerals,* Rx no. 287.

ANORTHOSITE — See Simon and Schuster's *Rocks and Minerals,* Rx no. 288.

OLIVINE GABBRO — See Simon and Schuster's *Rocks and Minerals,* Rx no. 286.

PYROXENITE — See Simon and Schuster's *Rocks and Minerals,* Rx no. 291.

HORNBLENDITE — See Simon and Schuster's *Rocks and Minerals,* Rx no. 292.

PERIDOTITE — See Simon and Schuster's *Rocks and Minerals,* Rx no. 295 and 296.

DUNITE — See Simon and Schuster's *Rocks and Minerals,* Rx no. 293.

The most common intrusive rocks fall between granite and granodiorite on the rock chart. The remaining rocks occur infrequently.

LAMPROPHYRE — A rock that is derived from silicic to intermediate plutons as dikes and small masses along the margins of the main intrusive body. It is dark colored with a variable composition, because it is made up of a variety of "leftovers" from the magmatic activity.

See Simon and Schuster's *Rocks and Minerals,* Rx no. 322.

CARBONATITE — Not included in the Igneous Rock Chart, carbonatite is a rare medium to coarse grained intrusive, predominantly carbonate in composition. Carbonatites occur as small intrusive bodies, often as dikes and dike swarms, closely associated with soda-rich intrusives such as nepheline syenite. Carbonatites are considered to have a deep magmatic origin, similar to the peridotite diamond pipes. Essential minerals include calcite and dolomite, with lesser feldspars (orthoclase and albite), nepheline, pyroxene, biotite and olivine. Some carbonatites contain a wide variety of accessory minerals including concentrations of rare earth minerals.

See Simon and Schuster's *Rocks and Minerals,* Rx no. 313.

It should be remembered that the Igneous Rock Chart is not complete, and is only enough to give a background. The study of rocks (petrology) is a specialty unto itself and far beyond the scope of this book.

See *Prospecting for Gemstones and Minerals,* 100-104, 137.

CHAPTER 4: Sedimentary Rocks

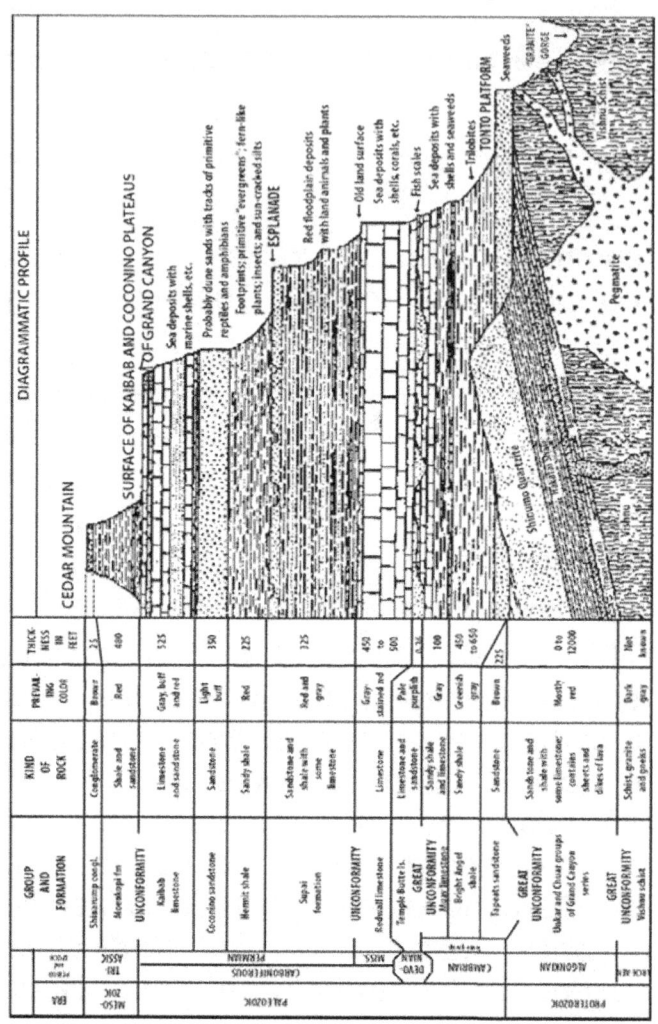

Diagrammatic cross-section of the Grand Canyon.
(From Field, R.M., *Geology — College Outline Series*, Barnes & Noble, 1951)

INTRODUCTION

Sedimentary rocks are formed by sedimentary processes which include the weathering and erosion of pre-existing rock, and the subsequent transportation, deposition and solidification, including precipitation, of the eroded material.

Don't confuse sediment, which is unconsolidated material such as sand and gravel, with sedimentary rock where the sand and gravel have been cemented into rock called sandstone and conglomerate.

The common and abundant materials of sedimentary rocks are few, consisting of quartz, feldspar, calcite, dolomite, clay minerals and micas.

The sedimentary cycle starts with mechanical and/or chemical weathering of pre-existing rocks. Mechanical weathering is the breakdown of rocks into smaller and smaller particles. Ice and frost action play an important role in mechanical weathering. Chemical weathering is the breaking and wearing down of rock by chemical reaction. Of the common minerals in igneous rocks, only quartz is highly resistant to weathering processes. Feldspars are less resistant than quartz, and may be chemically decomposed by prolonged weathering.

The cycle continues as the weathered rock material is eroded and transported to new localities. Erosion and transportation occur by means of gravity, water, wind and ice (glaciers). Common examples would be the muddy Colorado River and dust and sand storms.

Deposition occurs when water velocity suddenly decreases, such as when a river empties into a lake or ocean, or when wind subsides.

A different type of deposition occurs when elements chemically in solution in water encounter just the right chemical conditions and precipitate out. Limestones and dolomites form this way in warm shallow seas, sometimes accumulating thicknesses of thousands of feet over millions of years. Salt and gypsum deposits, commonly seen in the beds of dry lakes, form as the result of evaporation. As the volume of water in a freshwater lake decreases due to evaporation, the water becomes more and more concentrated in calcium, magnesium and other salts, until it reaches a point of supersaturation, and precipitation begins. The Great Salt Lake, once a freshwater lake, is an example.

Solidification ends the sedimentary rock forming cycle. When sands and gravels are cemented, SANDSTONES and CONGLOMERATES are formed. SHALES and SILTSTONES can be formed by compaction resulting from the weight of overlaying material. LIMESTONES and DOLOMITES, composed of the minerals calcite and dolomite respectfully, form as rocks as part of the chemical precipitate process.

See Golden *Rocks and Minerals,* pages 14-16.
See *Prospecting for Gemstones and Minerals,* pages 104-111.

Sedimentary rocks cover approximately 75 percent of the land area, of which some 80 percent are shales, 15 percent sandstones, and five percent are limestones (including dolomites). By far, most sedimentary rocks are marine in origin. Far less common are terrestrial sediments deposited in lakes and related to rivers, wind or glaciers.

Sedimentary rocks are most generally bedded in parallel layers or strata when formed. This parallel bedding or stratification is one of the best means of recognizing sedimentary formations from a distance.

See *Prospecting for Gemstones and Minerals,* page 110, figure 44; page 114, figure 48; page 116, figure 51; page 123, figure 57; page 231, figure 106.
See Simon and Schuster's *Rocks and Minerals,* photograph of Grand Canyon at page 431 and between Rx no. 322 and 323.

It should be remembered that the sedimentary rocks seen exposed on the surface today were formed millions of years ago below sea level and have been uplifted, possibly thousands of feet, by crustal forces and then eroded. During crustal uplift, sedimentary bedding, originally horizontal, may be tilted, folded, and faulted (broken or displaced). Be aware sedimentary rock formations do not necessarily have to appear as horizontal beds as seen in the photographs you have just reviewed. Also, a series of lava flows may have what appears to be horizontal bedding. With close observation of the rocks you should have little difficulty distinguishing sedimentary rock from lava flows.

With changing conditions of deposition, it is not uncommon to find different sedimentary rocks interbedded with each other. See Figure 4-1.

CLASSIFICATION OF SEDIMENTARY ROCKS

Sedimentary rocks are classified in two main subdivisions: clastic rocks, i.e., rocks composed of smaller mineral and rock fragments, and chemical precipitates.

See Golden *Rocks and Minerals,* pages 16 (center) and 17.
See *Prospecting for Gemstones and Minerals,* pages 111-116.

TABLE 4-1
Classification of Clastic Sedimentary Rocks

TEXTURE	COMPOSITION	ROCK NAME
Boulders, cobbles and pebbles	Rounded fragments of any rock type — quartz, quartzite, chert dominant	CONGLOMERATE
Coarse Grained (over 2mm)	Angular fragments of any rock type — quartz, quartzite chert dominant	BRECCIA
Sand Medium Grained (2mm to 1/16mm)	Quartz with minor accessory minerals Essentially pure quartz sand	QUARTZ SANDSTONE QUARTZITE
	Quartz with at least 25% feldspar	ARKOSE
	Quartz, rock fragments, and considerable clay ("dirty" sandstone)	GRAYWACKE
Fine Grained (1/16 mm to 1/256mm)	Quartz and clay minerals	SILTSTONE
Very Fine Grained (less than 1/256mm)	Quartz and clay minerals	SHALE (fissle with partings) CLAYSTONE (no partings)
Medium to Fine Grained	Volcanic Ash	TUFF

TABLE 4-2
Classification of Non-Clastic Sedimentary Rocks

ENVIRONMENT OF FORMATION	TEXTURE	COMPOSITION	ROCK NAME
SEA & LARGE LAKE	Fine to coarse grain	$CaCO_3$ (Calcite)	LIMESTONE
	Fossils & fossil fragments loosely cemented		COQUINA
	Abundant fossils in calcareous matrix		Fossiliferous LIMESTONE
	Shells of microscopic organisms, soft clay		CHALK
	Textures similar to those of limestone	$CaMg(CO_3)_2$ (Dolomite)	DOLOMITE
	Cryptocrystalline, dense	Silica	CHERT (nodules)
EVAPORITE	Crystalline	$CaCO_3$ $CaSO_4 \cdot 2H_2O$ $CaSO_4$ $NaCl$ KCl	LIMESTONE GYPSUM ANHYDRITE HALITE SYLVITE
HOT SPRINGS	Sometimes banded	$CaCO_3$ SiO_3	TRAVERTINE, TUFA, calcareous, and siliceous SINTER
OXIDATION	Banded Fe oxides	Fe oxides	Bog iron
REDUCING		Organic plants Fe & silica pyrite & marcasite	COAL, black carbonaceous SHALES
ACCUMULATION OF PLANTS & ANIMALS	Accumulation of diatoms, Accumulation of fish remains	Silica	DIATOMITE (diatomaceous earth)
		Phosphate	PHOSPHORITE

FIGURE 4-1
Hypothetical Sedimentary Sequence Illustration of Folded and Faulted Interbedded Sedimentary Rocks

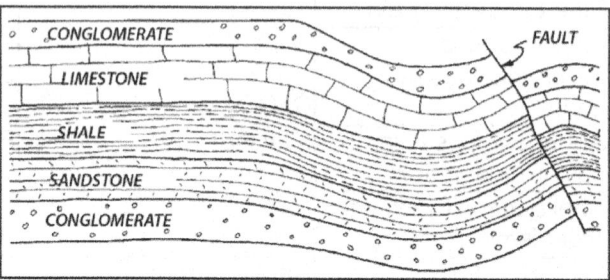

CLASTIC SEDIMENTARY ROCKS

In the clastic subdivision, rocks are further classified by the size of the mineral and rock fragments (see Table 4-1).

See Golden *Rocks and Minerals,* page 15 (top).

Rock composed of boulders and cobbles is called CONGLOMERATE if the boulders and cobbles are rounded, and BRECCIA if angular.

See Simon and Schuster's *Rocks and Minerals,* Rx nos. 323, 324 and 325.
See *Prospecting for Gemstones and Minerals,* page 112, figure 46.

SANDSTONE — Sand-sized particles, of which there are three main types:

1. QUARTZ SANDSTONE (QUARTZITE) — where quartz sand grains predominate.

See Simon and Schuster's *Rocks and Minerals,* Rx no. 327.
See *Prospecting for Gemstones and Minerals,* page 113, figure 47.

2. ARKOSE — composed mainly of quartz and greater than 25% feldspar grains, often pinkish in color.

See Simon and Schuster's *Rocks and Minerals,* Rx no. 328.

3. GRAYWACKE — often called "dirty" sandstone because it is a mixture of quartz and feldspar grains, other dark constituents, and clay. Often it is gray in color.

See Simon and Schuster's *Rocks and Minerals,* Rx no. 329.

SILTSTONE — made up of silt-sized particles.

SHALE — composed of clay-sized particles, showing platy partings in the rocks.

CLAYSTONE — composed of clay-sized particles without the platy partings.

See *Prospecting for Gemstones and Minerals,* page 116, figure 51.

Volcanic ash, which falls in lakes, consolidates to form TUFF, a special class of sedimentary rock.

See Simon and Schuster's *Rocks and Minerals,* Rx nos. 350 and 351.
See *Prospecting for Gemstones and Minerals,* page 94, figure 32, and page 212, figure 94.

CHEMICAL PRECIPITATES

Rocks of this subdivision are further classified by environment of formation.

LIMESTONE — the most common of the chemical precipitate rocks, forms in a shallow, warm sea environment. Varieties of limestone which are composed of the mineral calcite are numerous, ranging from plain "old" gray limestone to those containing numerous kinds of fossils.

See *Prospecting for Gemstones and Minerals,* page 117, figure 52, no. 4 (plain gray limestone).
See Simon and Schuster's *Rocks and Minerals,* Rx nos. 335, 338 and 339.

MARL — limestone mixed or interbedded with mudstone.

See Simon and Schuster's *Rocks and Minerals,* Rx no. 331.

DOLOMITE — composed of the mineral dolomite and similar to limestone, the only difference being that magnesium was available and combined with calcium and carbonate.

See Simon and Schuster's *Rocks and Minerals,* Rx nos. 340 and 341.

Under certain conditions, when silica is present, chert will form as nodules in limestone and dolomite beds.

EVAPORITE ENVIRONMENT AND DEPOSITS

* Minerals you should be able to identify.

As inland seas and lakes evaporate, the waters become supersaturated in certain elements. Generally, the first mineral to precipitate is calcite (limestone), followed by gypsum, anhydrite, halite, and sylvite.

See *Prospecting for Gemstones and Minerals,* pages 109-111, 121-122.

GYPSUM* — $CaSO_4 \cdot 2H_2O$.

See Simon and Schuster's *Rocks and Minerals,* mineral no. 122.
See Golden *Rocks and Minerals,* pages 238-239.

ANHYDRITE* — $CaSO_4$.

See Simon and Schuster's *Rocks and Minerals,* mineral no. 113.
See Golden *Rocks and Minerals,* page 238-239.

HALITE* — NaCl.

See Simon and Schuster's *Rocks and Minerals,* mineral no. 47.
See Golden *Rocks and Minerals,* pages 120-121.

SYLVITE — KCl.

See Simon and Schuster's *Rocks and Minerals,* mineral no. 48.
See Golden *Rocks and Minerals,* pages 120-121.

Where hot springs have injected some of the rarer elements, such as boron, into lake waters, interesting suites of minerals can occur. The borate deposits at Boron, California and the brines at Trona, California are examples.

BORAX — $Na_2B_4O_7 \cdot 10H_2O$. Borax is colorless. Oxidized, it is called tincalconite — chalk white in appearance.

See Simon and Schuster's *Rocks and Minerals,* mineral no. 109.
See Golden *Rocks and Minerals,* pages 152-153.

ULEXITE — $NaCaB_5O_9 \cdot 8H_2O$.

See Simon and Schuster's *Rocks and Minerals,* mineral no. 110.
See Golden *Rocks and Minerals,* pages 152-153.

COLEMANITE — $Ca_2B_6O_{11} \cdot 5H_2O$.

See Simon and Schuster's *Rocks and Minerals,* mineral no. 111.
See Golden *Rocks and Minerals,* pages 152-153.

KERNITE — $Na_2B_4O_7 \cdot 4H_2O$.

See Simon and Schuster's *Rocks and Minerals,* mineral no. 108.

TRONA — $Na_3(CO_3)HCO_3 \cdot 2H_2O$.

See Simon and Schuster's *Rocks and Minerals,* mineral no. 105.
See Golden *Rocks and Minerals,* pages 234-235.

CELESTITE — $SrSO_4$.

See Simon and Schuster's *Rocks and Minerals,* mineral no. 114.
See Golden *Rocks and Minerals,* pages 240-241.

HOT SPRINGS ENVIRONMENT

Very limited in area, hot spring environments show aprons and deposits of rocks composed of $CaCO_3$ with a variety of names: TRAVERTINE, TUFA, calcareous SINTER and ONYX. Rock composed of SiO_2 is called siliceous SINTER.

OXIDATION AND REDUCING ENVIRONMENTS

Where oxidizing conditions exist, silica and iron can precipitate in shallow seas or lakes. Bog iron deposits of GOETHITE and HEMATITE form in this way, as do beds of manganese.

See Simon and Schuster's *Rocks and Minerals,* Rx no. 345.
See *Prospecting for Gemstones and Minerals,* pages 122 (bottom)-123.

Where reducing conditions exist, conditions are favorable for the formation of coal, and sedimentary pyrite and marcasite, often related to black carbonaceous shales.

See Simon and Schuster's *Rocks and Minerals,* Rock nos. 346 and 347.
See *Prospecting for Gemstones and Minerals,* pages 123-124.

ACCUMULATION OF REMAINS OF PLANTS AND ANIMALS ENVIRONMENT AND DEPOSITS

Accumulations of plant and animal remains in shallow seas and lakes can form deposits of apatite, diatomaceous earth, chalk, coal and phosphorite.

See *Prospecting for Gemstones and Minerals,* pages 123-124.

APATITE* — $Ca_5(PO_4)_3(OH,F, Cl)$.

See Simon and Schuster's *Rocks and Minerals,* mineral no. 140.
See Golden *Rocks and Minerals,* page 246.

DIATOMITE — Forms from the accumulation of diatoms (one-celled plants) in silica rich lake waters. Deposits are scattered in the western United States.

See Simon and Schuster's *Rocks and Minerals,* Rx no. 342.

PHOSPHORITE — Forms from the accumulation of bones, fish and vertebrates. The Phosphoria Formation in the western United States is such a deposit.

See Simon and Schuster's *Rocks and Minerals,* Rx no. 344.

CHAPTER 5: Metamorphic Rocks

INTRODUCTION

The third and last major rock subdivision consists of rocks which have formed from pre-existing igneous or sedimentary, or even metamorphic, rocks. Pressure, heat and chemical activity have caused the original minerals to recrystallize and new minerals to form. The resulting metamorphic rocks depend upon the degree of metamorphism (which can be slight to strong), the degree of chemical activity, and the mineral composition of the original rock.

CLASSIFICATION OF METAMORPHIC ROCKS

Metamorphic rocks can be classified in several ways: contact metamorphic rocks and regional metamorphic rocks, or foliated and non-foliated (see Table 5-1). Contact metamorphic rocks form where magma (in the process of forming "granitic" type rocks) is intruded into overlying rocks. The high temperature along the intrusive contact, coupled with the associated chemical activity, can produce a contact metamorphic zone tens to hundreds of feet thick. This is especially true where limestone and dolomite are close to the contact, because they are chemically "ripe" for recrystallization and formation of new minerals.

See Golden *Rocks and Minerals,* page 13 (center) for a typical cross-section.

Limestone or dolomite contact metamorphic zones are a favorable host for ore-bearing solutions and deposits of magnetite, copper, molybdenite or tungsten. The silicated rock in the contact zone, originally limestone or dolomite, is called SKARN or TACTITE.

Regional metamorphism may occur across thousands of square miles. Pressure is much more dominant than in contact metamorphism. Regional metamorphism is related to tectonic forces causing continental plate movement, resulting in sinking of surface or near-surface rock masses deeper into the crust, and mountain building over long periods of time. This causes near-surface volcanic and sedimentary rocks to be folded, buckled, sheared and metamorphosed.

A feature common to regional metamorphic rocks is foliation, a texture related to the presence of directional forces, characterized by a general flattening of the minerals.

See Simon and Schuster's *Rocks and Minerals,* Rx nos. 353, 356, 362, 364 and 365.

For background information on metamorphic rocks:

See *Prospecting for Gemstones and Minerals,* pages I24-129.

See Simon and Schuster's *Rocks and Minerals,* pages 421 (bottom)-426 (center).

See Golden *Rocks and Minerals,* pages 10-13.

TABLE 5-1
Metamorphic Rock Chart

FOLIATED - GENERALLY REGIONAL METAMORPHISM

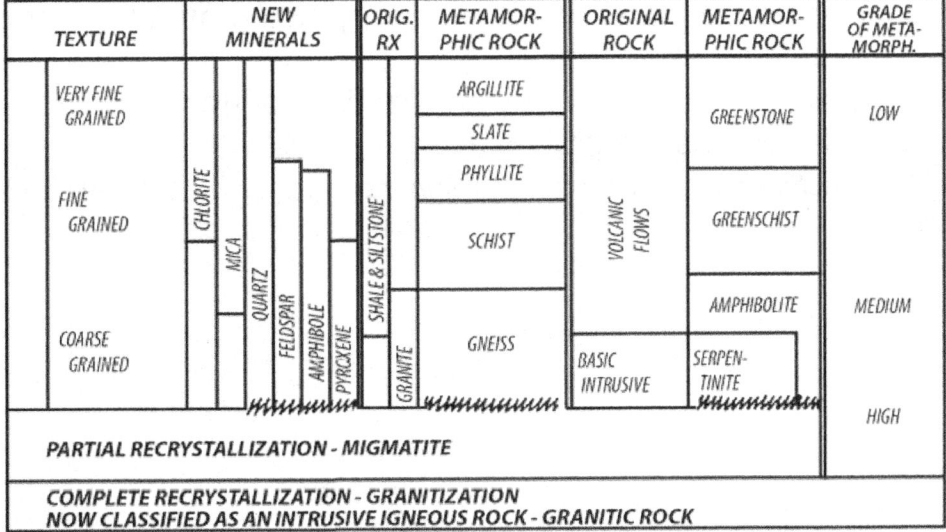

TEXTURE	NEW MINERALS	ORIG. RX	METAMOR-PHIC ROCK	ORIGINAL ROCK	METAMOR-PHIC ROCK	GRADE OF META-MORPH.
VERY FINE GRAINED	CHLORITE, MICA, QUARTZ, FELDSPAR, AMPHIBOLE, PYROXENE	SHALE & SILTSTONE / GRANITE	ARGILLITE	VOLCANIC FLOWS	GREENSTONE	LOW
			SLATE			
FINE GRAINED			PHYLLITE		GREENSCHIST	
			SCHIST			
					AMPHIBOLITE	MEDIUM
COARSE GRAINED			GNEISS	BASIC INTRUSIVE	SERPEN-TINITE	
						HIGH

PARTIAL RECRYSTALLIZATION - MIGMATITE

COMPLETE RECRYSTALLIZATION - GRANITIZATION
NOW CLASSIFIED AS AN INTRUSIVE IGNEOUS ROCK - GRANITIC ROCK

NONFOLIATED - REGIONAL & CONTACT METAMORPHISM

TEXTURE	COMPOSITION	ORIGINAL ROCK	METAMORPHIC ROCK	METAMOR. CLASS
COARSE	FRAGMENTS OF ANY ROCK TYPE	CONGLOMERATE	METACONGLOMERATE	REGIONAL & CONTACT
FINE TO COARSE	QUARTZ & SAND	SANDSTONE	METAQUARTZITE	REGIONAL & CONTACT
FINE	SILT & CLAY	SHALE OR SILTSTONE	HORNFELS	REGIONAL & CONTACT
MEDIUM TO COARSE	CALCITE OR DOLOMITE	LIMESTONE OR DOLOMITE	MARBLE	REGIONAL & CONTACT
FINE TO COARSE	(METASOMATISM-SOLUTIONS ADDED (W/Fe, Cu, Mo,W)		SKARN (CALC-SILICATE) TACTITE	CONTACT ONLY

REGIONAL METAMORPHIC ROCKS

Many variables exist in the formation of regional metamorphic rocks. Pressure, temperature and mineral composition of the original rocks can be combined in many combinations, yielding numerous varieties of metamorphic rocks.

Where there is complete recrystallization, a new granitic rock is formed by the process of granitization.

See *Prospecting for Gemstones and Minerals,* pages 129 (middle)-135, and 139.

TABLE 5-2
Regional Metamorphic Rocks

Original Rock	Grade of Metamorphism	Metamorphic Rock	Reference (See Simon & Schuster's *Rocks and Minerals*)
Conglomerate	Low-Medium	METACONGLOMERATE	
Quartzite or	Low	METAQUARTZITE	Rx No. 352
Sandstone	High	QUARTZITE GNEISS	
Siltstone	Medium	HORNFELS	Rx No. 374
Limestones & Dolomites	Low-Medium	MARBLE	Rx No. 371
Silty Limestone	Medium	MARBLE to CALC-SILICATE	Rx No. 375
Shale & Limestone	Very Low (baking)	ARGILLITE	Rx No. 330
	Low	SLATE	Rx No. 373 (poor ex.)
	Increasing	PHYLLITE	Rx No. 353
	Medium	SCHIST	Rx No. 354, 355, 357
	High	GNEISS	Rx No. 356
Volcanic	Low	GREENSTONE	
Volcanic & Mafic Intrusive	Medium	AMPHIBOLITE	Rx No. 362 & 363
All Above	High	MIGMATITE (partial recrystallization)	Rx No. 364, 365, 366 & 367

53

CONTACT METAMORPHIC ROCKS

Contact metamorphic rocks are generally nonfoliated and classified as follows:

TABLE 5-3
Contact Metamorphic Rocks

Original Rock	Metamorphic Rock	Reference (See Simon & Schuster's *Rocks and Minerals*)
Conglomerate	METACONGLOMERATE	
Quartzite and Sandstone	METAQUARTZITE	Rx No. 352
Shale or Siltstone	HORNFELS	Rx No. 374
Limestone or Dolomite	MARBLE SKARN (CALC-SILICATE) TACTITE	Rx No. 371 Rx No. 376

See *Prospecting for Gemstones and Minerals,* pages 135-137.

METAMORPHIC MINERALS

Temperature, pressure, and chemical composition of the original rock will control the metamorphic minerals formed. Essential elements involved in the metamorphic rock forming processes include calcium, sodium, silica and water.

Related in a general sense are the grade of metamorphism, facies, and index minerals, shown below.

Grade of Metamorphism	Metamorphic Facies	Index Minerals
Low-grade (150°-250°C)	Zeolite Glaucophane Schist Greenschist	Chlorite & Albite
Medium-grade (250°-450°C)	Hornfels Eclogite Amphibolite	Almandine & Epidote
High-grade (450°-700°C)	Granulite Migmatite	Staurolite & Kyanite

Metamorphic facies are all the rocks that have originated under temperature and pressure conditions so similar that a definite chemical composition has resulted in the same set of minerals. A discussion of metamorphic facies is beyond the scope of this book.

See Simon and Schuster's *Rocks and Minerals,* page 422 (top diagram).

FIGURE 5-1
Typical Cross-Section of a Contact Metamorphic Zone

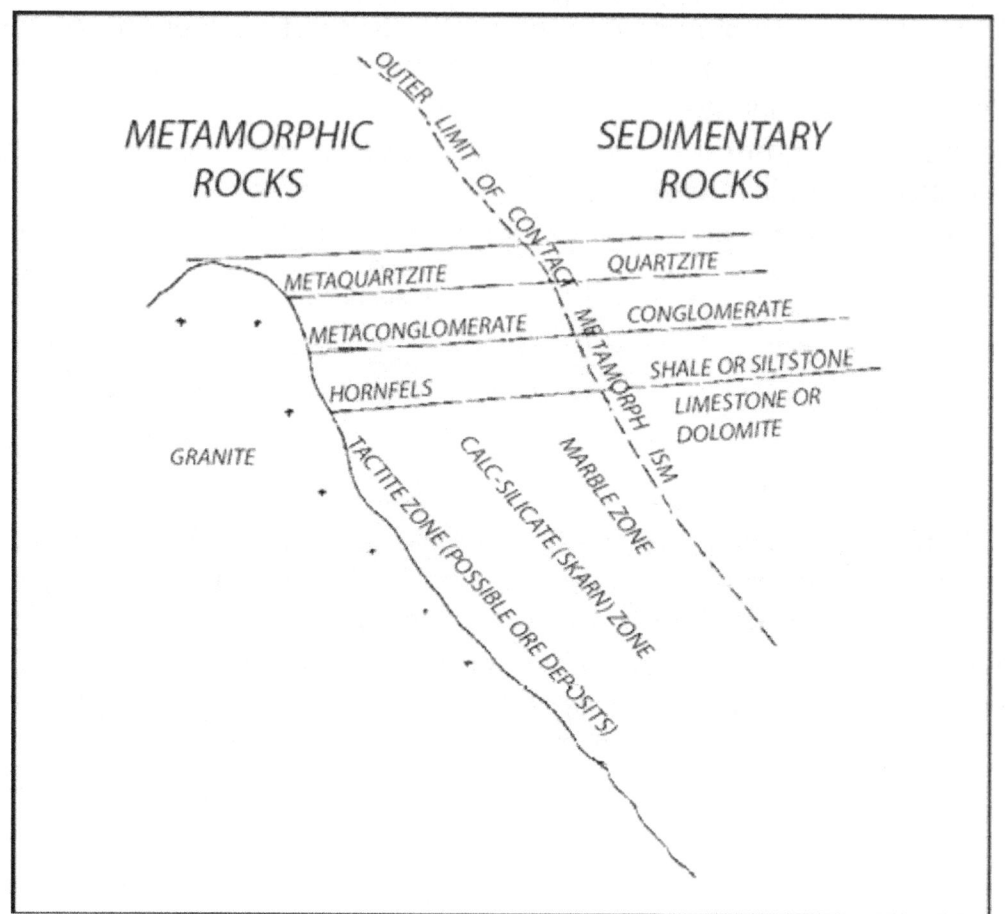

MINERALS FOUND IN REGIONAL METAMORPHIC ENVIRONMENTS

* Minerals you should be able to identify.

Listed generally as grade of metamorphism increases.

QUARTZ* — SiO_2. Low to high grade. Found in silica rich metamorphic rocks.

 See Simon and Schuster's *Rocks and Minerals,* mineral no. 244.
 See Golden *Rocks and Minerals,* page 206.

MUSCOVITE* — $KAl_2(Si_3Al)O_{10}(OH)_2$. Low to high grade. Found in greenschist and amphibolite.

 See Simon and Schuster's *Rocks and Minerals,* mineral no. 225.
 See Golden *Rocks and Minerals,* page 194.

CHLORITE* — $(Mg,Fe,Al)_6(Si,Al)_4O_{10}(OH)_8$. Low grade. Found in schist, metaquartzite, blueschist, amphibolite and gneiss. Associated with almandine and glaucophane.

 See Simon and Schuster's *Rocks and Minerals,* mineral no. 236, 237.
 See Golden *Rocks and Minerals,* page 200.

SERPENTINE* — $(Mg,Fe)_3Si_2O_5(OH)_4$. Low grade. Mg, Fe rich environment. Originating from mafic and ultramafic igneous rocks. Variety: CHRYSOTILE (Asbestos).

 See Simon and Schuster's *Rocks and Minerals,* mineral no. 239, 241.
 See Golden *Rocks and Minerals,* page 190.

WOLLASTONITE* — $CaSiO_3$. Low grade. Found in marbles and hornfels.

 See Simon and Schuster's *Rocks and Minerals,* mineral no. 213.
 See Golden *Rocks and Minerals,* page 180.

JADEITE* — $Na(Al,Fe^{+3})(SiO_3)_2$. Low to medium grade. Found in blueschists. Associated with glaucophane.

 See Simon and Schuster's *Rocks and Minerals,* mineral no. 196.
 See Golden *Rocks and Minerals,* page 180.

TREMOLITE* — $Ca_2Mg_5(Si_8O_{22})(OH)_2$. Low to medium grade. Found in serpentine and talc schist. Associated with magnesite and calcite.

See Simon and Schuster's *Rocks and Minerals,* mineral no. 204.
See Golden *Rocks and Minerals,* page 182.

ACTINOLITE* — $Ca_2(Mg,Fe)_5(Si_8O_{22})(OH)_2$. Low to medium grade. Found in greenstone and schist. Associated with albite, chlorite and epidote.

See Simon and Schuster's *Rocks and Minerals,* mineral no. 205.
See Golden *Rocks and Minerals,* page 182.

ANDALUSITE* — Al_2SiO_5. Low to medium grade. Found in schist and gneiss rich in Al and deficient in Ca, K, and Na. Associated with almandine, cordierite and muscovite.

See Simon and Schuster's *Rocks and Minerals,* mineral no. 167.
See Golden *Rocks and Minerals,* page 166.

SPESSARTITE* (garnet) — $Mn_3Al_2Si_3O_{12}$. Low to medium grade. Found in blueschist. Associated with quartz and riebeckite.

EPIDOTE* — $Ca_2(Al,Fe)_3Si_3O_{12}(OH)$. Medium grade. Found in amphibolite and blueschist. Associated with almandine and actinolite.

See Simon and Schuster's *Rocks and Minerals,* mineral no. 181.
See Golden *Rocks and Minerals,* page 160.

TALC* — $Mg_3Si_4O_{10}(OH)_2$. Medium grade. Found in dolomitic marbles and schists. Associated with tremolite and magnesite.

See Simon and Schuster's *Rocks and Minerals,* mineral no. 224.
See Golden *Rocks and Minerals,* page 192.

DIOPSIDE* — $CaMgSi_2O_6$. Medium grade. Found in hornfels. Associated with phlogopite and actinolite.

See Simon and Schuster's *Rocks and Minerals,* mineral no. 193.
See Golden *Rocks and Minerals,* page 176.

ALMANDINE* (ALMONDITE) (garnet) — $Fe_3Al_2Si_3O_{12}$. Medium grade. Found in schist. Associated with andalusite.

See Simon and Schuster's *Rocks and Minerals,* mineral no. 161.
See Golden *Rocks and Minerals,* page 162.

UVAROVITE* (garnet) — $Ca_3Cr_2Si_3O_{12}$. Medium grade. Found in serpentinized peridotite. Associated with chromite.

See Simon and Schuster's *Rocks and Minerals,* mineral no. 163.
See Golden *Rocks and Minerals,* page 162.

SILLIMANITE * — Al_2SiO_5. Medium to high grade. Found in schist and gneiss. Associated with almandine, biotite and quartz.

See Simon and Schuster's *Rocks and Minerals,* mineral no. 166.
See Golden *Rocks and Minerals,* page 166.

PHLOGOPITE — $K(Mg,Fe)_3(Al,Si_3)O_{10}(OH)_2$. Medium to high grade. Found in dolomitic marble and serpentine.

See Simon and Schuster's *Rocks and Minerals,* mineral no. 229.
See Golden *Rocks and Minerals,* page 196.

PLAGIOCLASE* — $(Na,Ca)(AlSi)_4O_8$ (with the exception of anorthosite). Medium to high grade. Found in schist and gneiss.

See Simon and Schuster's *Rocks and Minerals,* mineral nos. 258, 259.
See Golden *Rocks and Minerals,* page 218.

MICROCLINE* — $KAlSi_3O_8$. Medium to high grade. Found in gneiss.

See Simon and Schuster's *Rocks and Minerals,* mineral no. 255.
See Golden *Rocks and Minerals,* page 214.

PYROPE* (garnet) — $Mg_3Al_2Si_3O_{12}$. High grade. Found in serpentized peridotite, deficient in silica.

See Simon and Schuster's *Rocks and Minerals,* mineral no. 160.
See Golden *Rocks and Minerals,* page 162.

KYANITE* — Al_2SiO_5. High grade. Found in schist, gneiss, amphibolite and eclogite. Associated with quartz, garnet, staurolite, and biotite.

See Simon and Schuster's *Rocks and Minerals,* mineral no. 168.
See Golden *Rocks and Minerals,* page 166.

STAUROLITE* — $(Fe,Mg,Zn)_2Al_9Si_4O_{23}(OH)$. High grade. Found in schist and gneiss. Associated with garnet, kyanite and sillimenite.

See Simon and Schuster's *Rocks and Minerals,* mineral no. 170.
See Golden *Rocks and Minerals,* page 166.

CORUNDUM* — Al_2O_3. High grade. Found in marble, schist and granulite, rich in Al and deficient in silica.

See Simon and Schuster's *Rocks and Minerals,* mineral no. 64.
See Golden *Rocks and Minerals,* page 134.

GRAPHITE* — C. High grade. Formed as the result of carbonization of organic substances.

See Simon and Schuster's *Rocks and Minerals,* mineral no. 10.
See Golden *Rocks and Minerals,* page 76.

ORTHOCLASE* — $KAlSi_3O_8$. High grade. Found in gneiss and migmatite.

See Simon and Schuster's *Rocks and Minerals,* mineral no. 254.
See Golden *Rocks and Minerals,* page 216.
See *Prospecting for Gemstones and Minerals,* page 129.

MINERALS FOUND IN CONTACT METAMORPHIC ENVIRONMENTS

PLAGIOCLASE* (anorthite only) — $CaAl_2Si_2O_8$. Found in hornfels. Associated with calcite and spinel.

See Simon and Schuster's *Rocks and Minerals,* mineral no. 259.
See Golden *Rocks and Minerals,* page 220.

ANDRADITE* (garnet) — $Ca_3Fe_2Si_3O_{12}$. Found in hornfels and skarn. Associated with calcite and hedenbergite.

See Simon and Schuster's *Rocks and Minerals,* mineral no. 164.
See Golden *Rocks and Minerals,* page 162.

GROSSULAR* (garnet) — $Ca_3Al_2Si_3O_{12}$. Found in hornfels. Associated with wollastonite, calcite and vesuvianite.

> See Simon and Schuster's *Rocks and Minerals,* mineral no. 162.
> See Golden *Rocks and Minerals,* page 162.

The following minerals are found in marbles, hornfels, calcsilicates and skarns, and are described in detail in the previous Regional Metamorphic Mineral section of this book.

ACTINOLITE — Associated with epidote.

ALMANDINE — Associated with andalusite.

ANDALUSITE

DIOPSIDE — Associated with phlogopite and actinolite.

EPIDOTE — Associated with chlorite and actinolite.

PHLOGOPITE

SILLIMENITE

STAUROLITE

TALC — Associated with tremolite.

TREMOLITE

WOLLASTONITE

The following minerals are found in greenstones:

ACTINOLITE

CHLORITE

EPIDOTE

MINERAL DEPOSITS OF METAMORPHIC ORIGIN

Regional and contact metamorphic environments offer excellent mineral collecting potential. Regionally, metamorphosed rocks can yield garnet, corundum, spinel, jadeite and other gemstones. The degree of regional metamorphism and original rock type controls the mineral suites that will develop.

See *Prospecting for Gemstones and Minerals,* page 129 (top).

Contact metamorphic environments offer potential for garnet, marble and other minerals.

Mineral deposits include talc, asbestos, graphite, roofing and building stone (slate and marble), and abrasive garnet.

See *Prospecting for Gemstones and Minerals,* pages 176 and 222-226 (bottom).

Iron ore beds of the Mesabi Range in the Great Lakes region consist of alternating bands of red jasper and iron oxides. The rocks of these beds are JASPILITE and TACONITE.

See Simon and Schuster's *Rocks and Minerals,* Rx. no. 336.
See *Prospecting for Gemstones and Minerals,* pages 134 and 139.

PART III — Mineral Deposits
CHAPTER 6: Magmatic Deposits

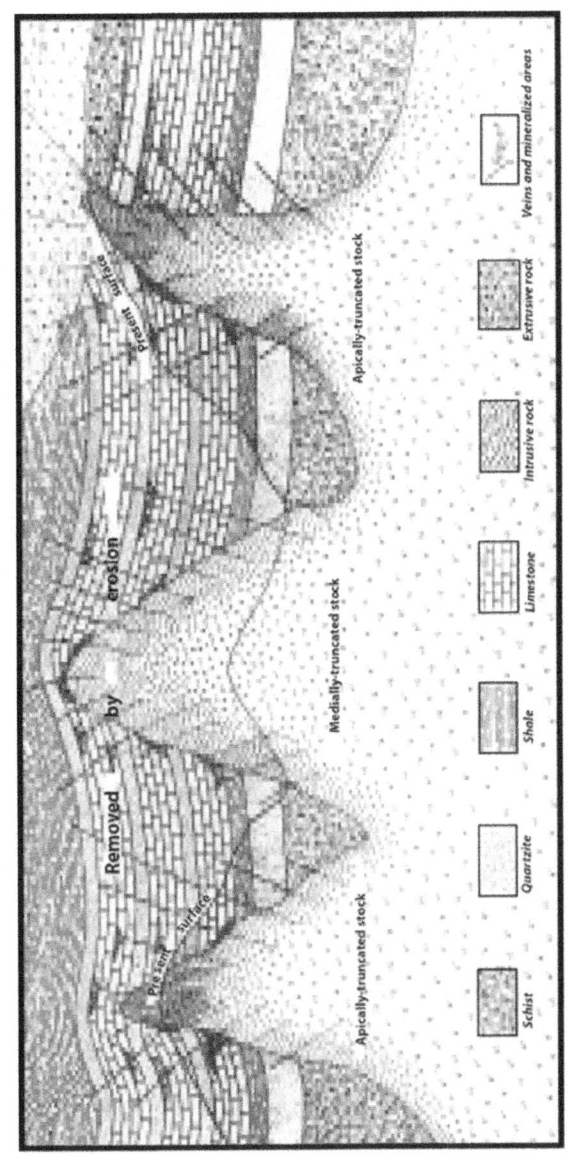

Section through an intrusive body showing zones of mineralization and present day surface.
(From Butler, B.S., *Economic Geology,* Vol. 10, 1915)

INTRODUCTION

A mineral deposit is any valuable mass of rock or mineral. To fully appreciate and benefit from prospecting, a knowledge of mineral deposits and their geologic environments is necessary. Mineral deposits can be divided into two general topics for discussion: the nonmetallic or industrial minerals (including gemstone deposits), and the metallic mineral deposits.

Examples of nonmetallic deposits include the evaporite and borate minerals discussed in the Sedimentary Rock section, barite, clays, garnets, limestone, quartz and silica minerals, topaz, ruby, tourmaline and others. Metallic deposits include those containing iron, copper, lead, zinc, gold, silver, and other metals.

There are a number of ways mineral deposits can be classified. The classification presented here is based on a combination of rock environment in general, and type of occurrence, starting with the igneous process and then generally following the petrogenic (formation of rocks) cycle as presented on page 423 of Simon and Schuster's *Rocks and Minerals*. The study of mineral deposits is extensive and complex, and only a very general outline will be presented here. It should, however, give enough basic background so you will be able to continue the study if you so desire.

MINERAL DEPOSITS RELATED TO INTRUSIVE IGNEOUS ROCKS

Numerous metallic and nonmetallic mineral deposits are directly related to intrusive igneous rocks. A typical magma melt starts with the following constituents: calcium, magnesium, iron, aluminum, potassium, sodium, silicon, oxygen, hydrogen, titanium, sulphur, the rare and precious metal elements, and other elements. Remember, the first eight elements listed make up 98.59 percent of the earth's crust; the remaining elements are rare indeed.

Intrusive igneous rocks originate in two general ways. Primary magma, basaltic in composition, originates as the result of partial melting of the upper mantle just beneath the crustal boundary. This basaltic magma is the source of most of the extrusive basalt lava flows found on land and in the oceans, most of the mafic and intermediate intrusive rocks, and smaller granite intrusives. The second way is called granitization where pre-existing rocks are recrystallized in a solid state.

Intrusion, remelting and recrystallization of magma produces residual hydrothermal solutions rich in the metal elements necessary for the formation of contact metamorphic deposits, mineralized veins and replacement deposits, and will be discussed in a later section.

BOWEN'S REACTION SERIES

The theory of what happens as a basaltic magma cools and crystallizes was developed by N.L. Bowen. Bowen's Reaction Series shows the stages of magmatic crystallization where interrupted. Field observations confirm the Reaction Series in general; however, the uninterrupted crystallization of a magma is somewhat rare, and many variations can occur. An understanding of the Reaction Series will help explain igneous rock classification, and its relationship to mineral deposits. The Reaction Series presented here has been expanded somewhat for purposes of clarity. See Figure 6-1.

FIGURE 6-1
Bowen's Reaction Series

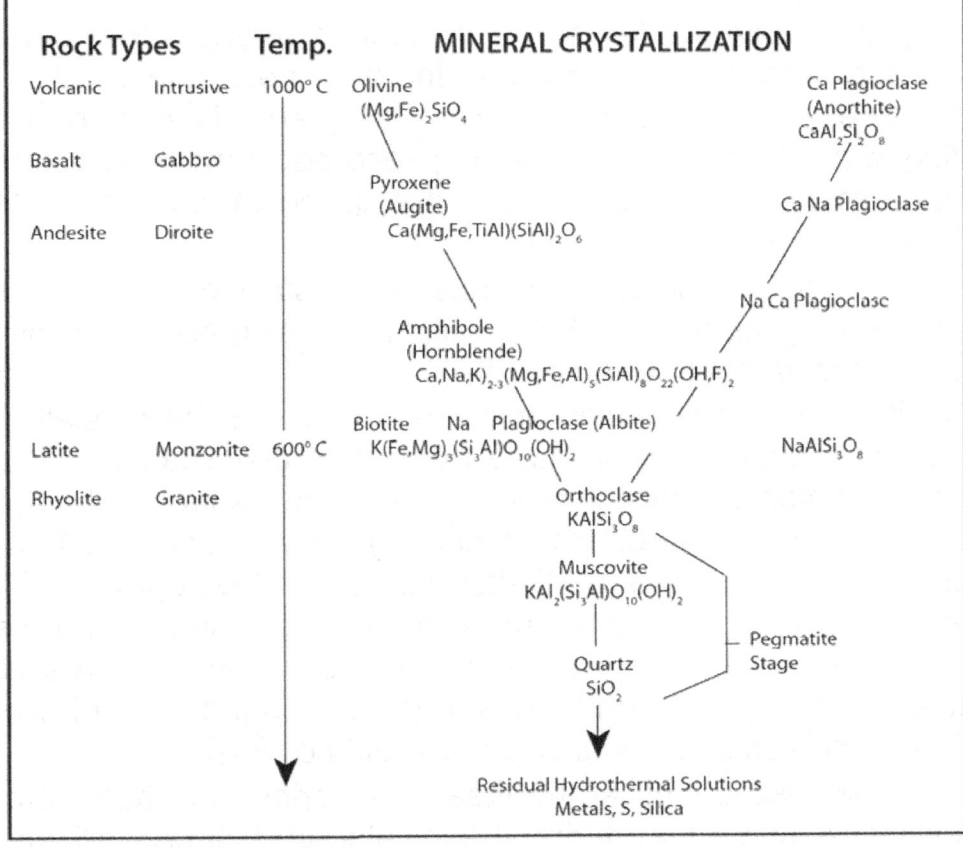

BOWEN'S REACTION SERIES
TYPICAL BASALTIC MAGMA MELT
Start with: Ca, Mg, Fe, Al, K, Na, Si, O, H, Ti, S, Au, Ag, Ca, Pb, Zn, Mo, W and other metals
(NOTE: Ten most abundant elements in earth's crust. See Chapter 1.

Rock Types		Temp.	MINERAL CRYSTALLIZATION	
Volcanic	Intrusive	1000° C	Olivine $(Mg,Fe)_2SiO_4$	Ca Plagioclase (Anorthite) $CaAl_2Sl_2O_8$
Basalt	Gabbro			
			Pyroxene (Augite) $Ca(Mg,Fe,TiAl)(SiAl)_2O_6$	Ca Na Plagioclase
Andesite	Diroite			
				Na Ca Plagioclase
			Amphibole (Hornblende) $Ca,Na,K)_{2-3}(Mg,Fe,Al)_5(SiAl)_8O_{22}(OH,F)_2$	
			Biotite Na Plagioclase (Albite) $K(Fe,Mg)_3(Si_3Al)O_{10}(OH)_2$	$NaAlSi_3O_8$
Latite	Monzonite	600° C		
Rhyolite	Granite		Orthoclase $KAlSi_3O_8$	
			Muscovite $KAl_2(Si_3Al)O_{10}(OH)_2$	
			Quartz SiO_2	Pegmatite Stage

Residual Hydrothermal Solutions
Metals, S, Silica

In theory, if basaltic magma crystallization is undisturbed, olivine and the plagioclase anorthite are first to crystallize at about 1,000°C. As the temperature slowly cools, the olivine crystals will react chemically with the remaining melt and be resorbed, forming a new mineral, augite (pyroxene), which will react chemically with the remaining melt and be resorbed, forming a new mineral, hornblende (amphibole), which will then react chemically with the remaining melt and be resorbed, forming the new mineral, biotite.

During the many hundreds and thousands of years that olivine is crystallizing and being resorbed, forming new minerals as the temperature of the magma cools, the plagioclase anorthite is reacting with the melt, not by being resorbed, but by the crystals taking on more and more sodium while giving up calcium, until the plagioclase albite is formed.

At about 600°C, the last minerals to crystallize are orthoclase, muscovite, and quartz, if silica is still available. If none is available, igneous rocks without quartz result.

In reality, magmatic concentration may occur or the crystallization may be interrupted at any stage by crustal disturbance ultimately causing intrusion and/or extrusion, and related sudden changes in temperature or pressure. Rapid cooling may result, which would freeze the magma in a particular stage of development. These features can be observed in the form of dikes, sills, laccoliths, or lava flows. We see it in the rocks with porphyritic textures (large crystals of earlier formed minerals in a fine groundmass of crystals whose growth has been quenched by rapid cooling).

Let us now take a look at the Reaction Series and theorize some disruptions. Assume that during the initial stages of crystallization of olivine or the plagioclase anorthite, magmatic segregation occurs followed by a sudden change in conditions whereby the olivine or the anorthite is injected into the surrounding rocks where rapid cooling follows. The rock formed upon cooling is DUNITE, composed essentially of the mineral olivine, or the rock

ANORTHOSITE, composed essentially of the mineral anorthite. If the magma itself were to quickly cool at this initial stage, the resulting rocks would be gabbroic in composition.

The same general explanation can be used to describe rocks such as PYROXENITES, AMPHIBOLITES, and the other intermediate and silicic igneous rocks found in the Classification of Igneous Rocks.

> See Simon and Schuster's *Rocks and Minerals,* The Igneous Process, pages 415-419.
>
> See *Prospecting for Gemstones and Minerals,* pages 140-143.

MINERALS RELATED TO COOLING MAGMA

* Minerals you should be able to identify.

Mineral deposits of chromium, platinum and nickel are directly associated with mafic and intermediate intrusive igneous rocks as disseminations or segregations.

CHROMITE — $FeCr_2O_4$. Occurs in mafic intrusive rocks.

> See Simon and Schuster's *Rocks and Minerals,* mineral no. 60.
>
> See Golden *Rocks and Minerals,* page 140.

PENTLANDITE — $(Fe,Ni)_9S_8$. Occurs in mafic intrusive rocks.

> See Simon and Schuster's *Rocks and Minerals,* mineral no. 16.
>
> See Golden *Rocks and Minerals,* page 100.

PLATINUM * — Pt. Occurs in mafic intrusive rocks.

> See Simon and Schuster's *Rocks and Minerals,* mineral no. 6.
>
> See Golden *Rocks and Minerals,* page 74.
>
> See *Prospecting for Gemstones and Minerals,* page 228.

DIAMOND* — C. Occurs in kimberlite pipes (altered peridotite).

> See Simon and Schuster's *Rocks and Minerals,* mineral no. 11.
>
> See Golden *Rocks and Minerals,* page 76.
>
> See *Prospecting for Gemstones and Minerals,* pages 226 (bottom)-228 (top).

PYRRHOTITE * — FeS. Associated with pentlandite, slightly magnetic.

See Simon and Schuster's *Rocks and Minerals,* mineral no. 22.
See Golden *Rocks and Minerals,* page 100.

ILMENITE* — FeTiO$_3$. Slightly magnetic.

See Simon and Schuster's *Rocks and Minerals,* mineral no. 66.
See Golden *Rocks and Minerals,* page 136.

PEGMATITES

As the end phase of magmatic crystallization approaches, the residual melt becomes more concentrated in silica and water. Under special conditions, some of the solutions and volatiles may be squeezed into fissures and form pegmatites. Pegmatites are characterized by large to extremely large crystals, and can be classified as simple or complex. Simple pegmatites consist of orthoclase and quartz, and often muscovite, and are generally related to magmas formed through granitization.

Complex pegmatites, in addition to orthoclase, quartz, and muscovite, contain crystals of some or all of the following: tourmaline, topaz, spodumene, beryl and other gemstone minerals. Complex pegmatites are related to basaltic magmas where there is a concentration during crystallization of volatile substances, such as fluorine, boron, chlorine, along with iron and tin, in addition to the residual solutions rich in silica and water.

See Simon and Schuster's *Rocks and Minerals,* Rx. no. 320.
See *Prospecting for Gemstones and Minerals,* pages 143-149 (bottom) and
    181-203.

MINERALS RELATED TO PEGMATITES

* Minerals you should be able to identify.

Minerals and gemstones common to simple and complex pegmatites are as follows: (quartz, orthoclase and muscovite were covered in the Igneous Rock Forming Minerals in Chapter 2).

TOURMALINE* — Complex formula.

See Simon and Schuster's *Rocks and Minerals,* mineral no. 190.
See Golden *Rocks and Minerals,* pages 170-171.

BERYL* — $Be_3Al_2Si_6O_{18}$

See Simon and Schuster's *Rocks and Minerals,* mineral no. 188.
See Golden *Rocks and Minerals,* pages 172-173.

TOPAZ* — $Al_2SiO_4(F,OH)_2$

See Simon and Schuster's *Rocks and Minerals,* mineral no. 169.
See Golden *Rocks and Minerals,* page 166.

SPODUMENE — $LiAlSi_2O_6$

See Simon and Schuster's *Rocks and Minerals,* mineral no. 140.
See Golden *Rocks and Minerals,* page 246.

APATITE * — $Ca_5(PO_4)_3(OH,F,Cl)$

See Golden *Rocks and Minerals,* mineral no. 140.
See Simon and Schuster's *Rocks and Minerals,* page 246.

URANINITE (PITCHBLENDE) — UO_2. Radioactive.

See Simon and Schuster's *Rocks and Minerals,* mineral no. 81.
See Golden *Rocks and Minerals,* page 146.
See *Prospecting for Gemstones and Minerals,* pages 204 (bottom)-205 (middle).

It should be remembered that pegmatites are rare. Most granitic intrusives do not have associated pegmatites because of the special conditions required for their formation. Most pegmatites that occur are of the simple type and the complex pegmatites are few.

CHAPTER 7: Hydrothermal Deposits

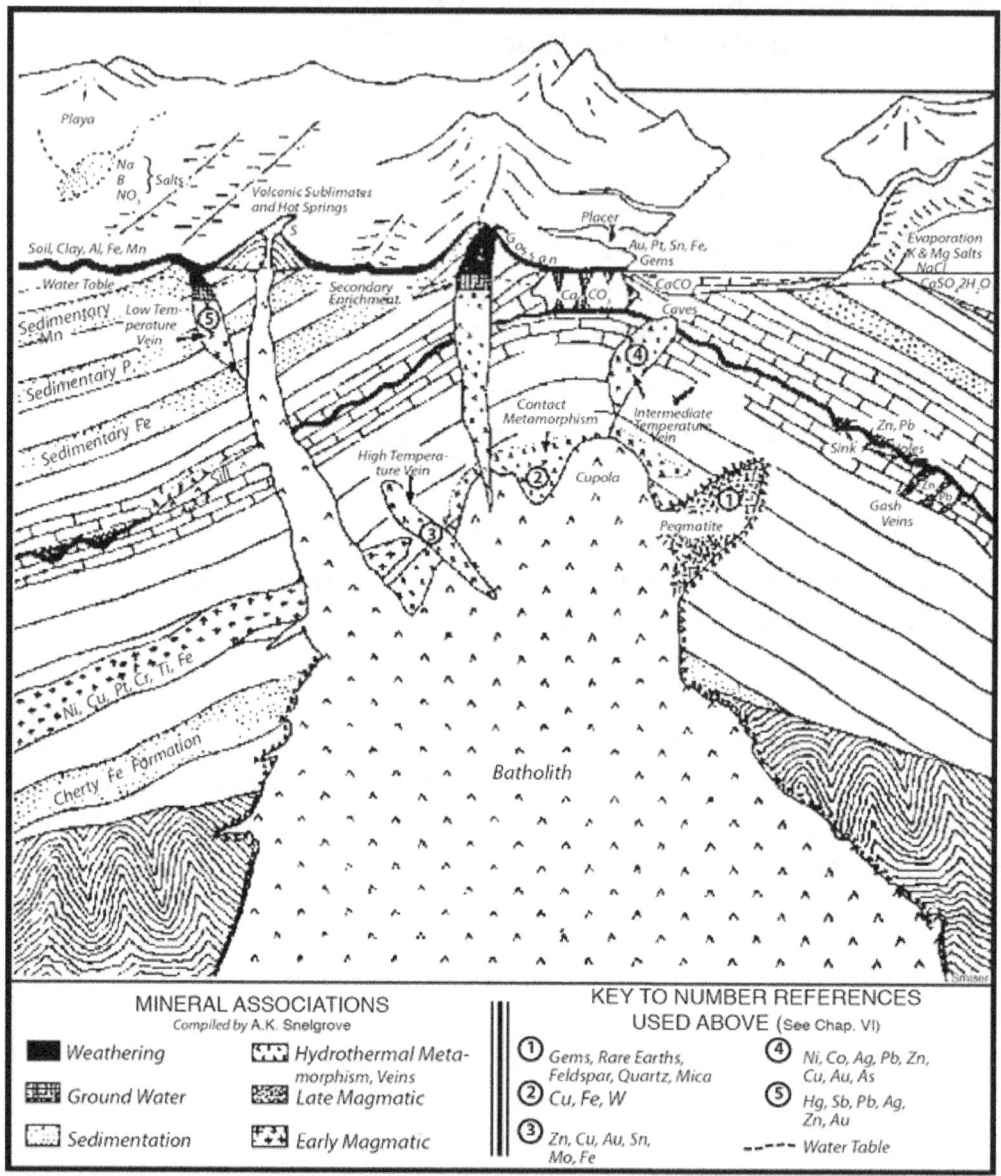

Early diagrammatic illustration of the origin of ore deposits.
(From Field, *R.M., Geology* — **College Outline Series,**

Barnes & Noble, Inc., 1951)

INTRODUCTION

The origin of the base and precious metal ions carried in hydrothermal solutions has long been open to debate. Metal ions are and were disseminated in the earth's mantle. Within convection cells in the mantle the ions are slowly transported toward the crust, concentrating over millions and hundreds of millions of years. Transport into the crust is at least in part by volcanic activity with roots into the mantle. Within the crust the metal ions have likely been subjected to several periods of concentration and reconcentration in the continuing geochemical cycle: rock formation, erosion, transportation and deposition, metamorphism and granitization.

Hydrothermal ("hot water") solutions can originate in several different geologic environments. Magmas, discussed in chapters 3 and 5, can be a major source of these solutions. Mineral deposits formed from magmatic hydrothermc-silver, and base and precious metal veins.

Studies in the last 20 years show an important relationship between certain types of mineralization, including massive sulphide deposits, and hydrothermal solutions derived from volcanic activity in volcanic belts related to crustal plate boundaries. Many deposits in this environment formed when metal ion-bearing hydrothermal solutions mixed with ground water or sea water.

Hydrothermal solutions can also form from rocks subjected to regional metamorphic processes. Base and precious metal ions are remobilized along with water from hydrous minerals which are heated and recrystallized into new minerals.

HYDROTHERMAL SOLUTIONS

The remaining liquid in the magma chambers, after crystallization of the great volume of silicate minerals, contains the metal ions for which we ultimately prospect. These hydrothermal solutions, or "juices," remaining determine the type of mineralization that will result. The hydrothermal phase may be well developed or poorly developed. It is necessary to look for evidence of the hydrothermal solution chemistry and its contents of metal ions.

For example, if hydrothermal solutions are rich in silica with a very small concentration of base or precious metal ions, essentially barren quartz veins would be expected. If the hydrothermal solutions contained no copper or gold ions, there would be no copper or gold minerals found.

Ideally, we want to start with a "juicy" magma which will produce a well-developed hydrothermal phase. Factors controlling hydrothermal mineralization include:

1. Chemistry of the magma and type of emplacement;
2. Quantity and chemistry of the hydrothermal solutions;
3. Temperature and pressure conditions;
4. Plumbing system for the solutions to travel along, including shattering, fracturing, shearing and faulting;
5. Reactivity of the surrounding rocks to the hydrothermal solutions.

Temperature and pressure conditions associated with emplacement of the magma during the final stages of crystallization control whether the hydrothermal solutions are in a liquid or gaseous phase. Delicate changes in temperature and pressure can cause the liquid phase to become gaseous and then liquid again. This can control the development of the contact metamorphic zone surrounding a cooling magma.

Well developed contact metamorphic zones showing skarns and tactites form as the result of metasomatism, where chemical reaction occurs between the gaseous hydrothermal phase originating from the magma and surrounding limestones and dolomites.

Generally, the mineral suites originating from hydrothermal solutions are temperature controlled. High temperature mineral suites, i.e., minerals that will form only at high temperatures, are found usually at depth within intrusive igneous rocks and in the contact metamorphic zone. Note that with few exceptions, the high temperature mineral suites consist of oxides. Predominantly sulphide mineralization begins as the intermediate temperature mineral suite range is approached.

Intermediate and low temperature mineral suites are deposited as the hydrothermal solutions work their way out, away from their source, cooling along the way. Our classification will follow the cooling hydrothermal solutions from the crystallizing magma, outward.

See *Prospecting for Gemstones and Minerals,* pages 152-153.
See Golden *Rocks and Minerals,* pages 82-83.

Metal zoning over a large area within a mining district may occur in a general sense, with molybdenum, copper and gold found close to the intrusive, and zinc, lead and silver mineralization found as one works out from the intrusive. See Figure 7-1.

FIGURE 7-1
Hydrothermal Mineral Zoning
Including Related Minerals

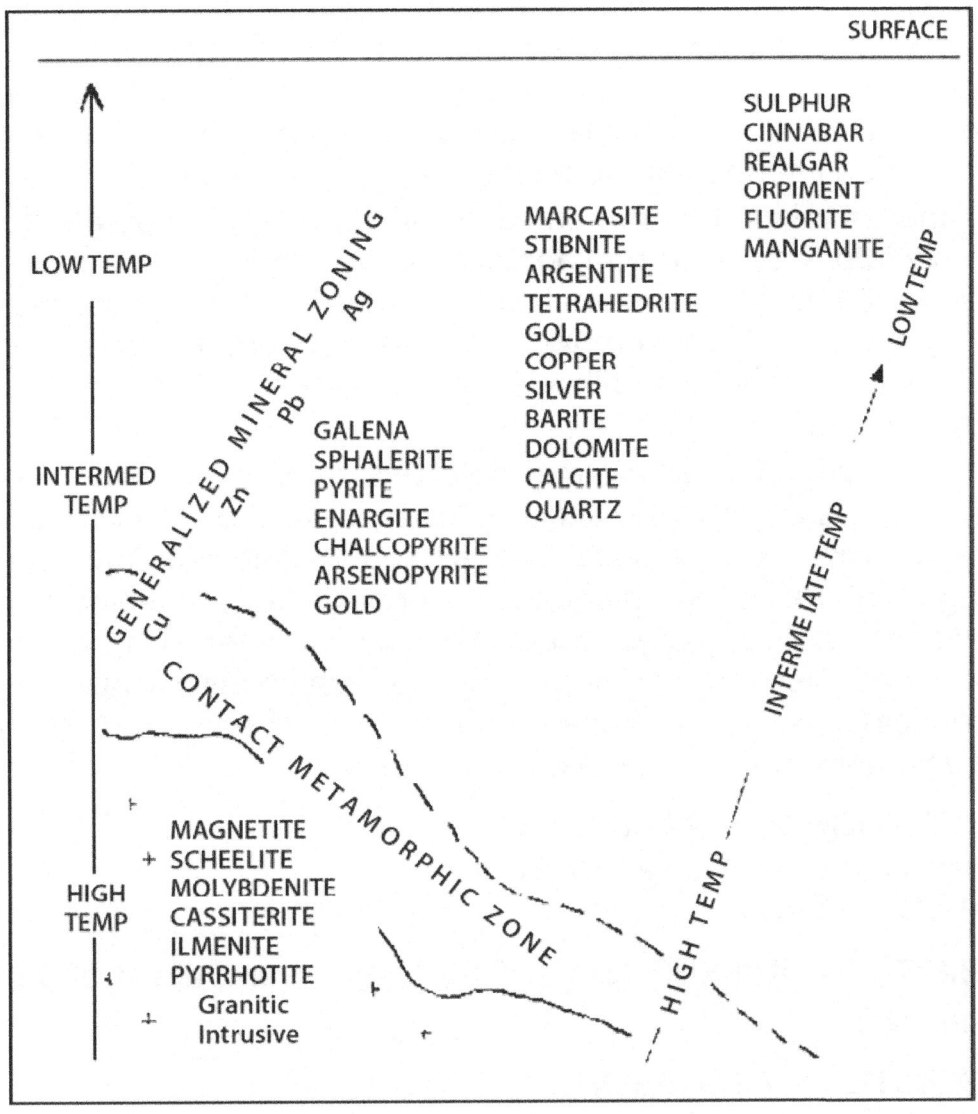

Hydrothermal solutions and mineralization occurs as described in a general sense. However, hydrothermal solutions may "pulse" several times over a substantial time period resulting in a "telescoping" of mineralization, that is, where different mineral suites overlap. An example is where the first period of mineralization produces a high temperature suite of minerals and a later second period of mineralization in the same place but under cooler conditions, produces an intermediate temperature suite of minerals.

It should also be remembered that high temperature and intermediate temperature mineralization usually occurs at depths as great as 5,000 feet and that subsequent uplift and erosion over millions of years has removed the overlying rocks to a position where we see the mineralization at the present day surface. See Figure 8-1, herein.

Well developed hydrothermal solutions often react with the host rock they pass through, altering the minerals of those rocks. In granitic rocks, feldspars can be altered to kaolinite and sericite, giving the rocks a "bleached" appearance. Amphiboles and pyroxenes can be altered to chlorite (chloritic alteration), giving the rock a greenish tinge. There may be related silicification of the surrounding rocks. The trained eye can spot these alteration halos and use them to zero in on exploration targets.

ALTERATION MINERALS

* Minerals you should be able to identify.

QUARTZ — SiO_2.

SERICITE* — $KAl_3Si_2O_5(OH)_2$. Silky luster, fine-grained and mica-like in habit.

KAOLINITE* — $Al_2Si_2O_5(OH)_4$.

See Simon and Schuster's *Rocks and Minerals,* mineral no. 238.
See Golden *Rocks and Minerals,* page 188.

CHLORITE* — $(Mg,Fe,Al)_6(Si,Al)_4O_{10}(OH)_8$.

See Golden *Rocks and Minerals,* page 200.

HIGH TEMPERATURE MINERALS

* Minerals you should be able to identify.

High temperature (hypothermal) hydrothermal mineralization will be closely associated in time and space with the parent magma, which provides the heat and hydrothermal solutions. Mineralization will occur as disseminations in stockworks of quartz veins, veins and replacements.

Deposits of tin, molybdenum and tungsten are of this type found in the outer parts of the magma, contact metamorphic zone and nearby invaded sedimentary and volcanic rocks.

Ore Minerals

CASSITERITE* — SnO_2. Disseminated in greisen (altered granite).

See Simon and Schuster's *Rocks and Minerals,* mineral no. 72.
See Golden *Rocks and Minerals,* page 144.

MOLYBDENITE* — MoS_2. Very soft with a platy appearance. Can occur in large, low-grade deposits as disseminations and veinlets in quartz stockworks.

See Simon and Schuster's *Rocks and Minerals,* mineral no. 37.
See Golden *Rocks and Minerals,* page 88.

SCHEELITE* — $CaWO_4$. Pale blue under the ultraviolet lamp. Generally found as disseminations in, and/or close to the contact metamorphic zone.

See Simon and Schuster's *Rocks and Minerals,* mineral no. 126.
See Golden *Rocks and Minerals,* page 256.

MAGNETITE* — $FeFe_2O_4$. Strongly magnetic. Occurs as disseminations and/or massive bodies in and close to the contact metamorphic zone.

See Simon and Schuster's *Rocks and Minerals,* mineral no. 58.
See Golden *Rocks and Minerals,* page 140.

GOLD* — Au.

See Simon and Schuster's *Rocks and Minerals,* mineral no. 3.
See Golden *Rocks and Minerals,* page 70.

Gangue Minerals

Gangue minerals include minerals listed under Pegmatites, and minerals listed under Contact Metamorphic Minerals.

INTERMEDIATE TEMPERATURE MINERALS

* Minerals you should be able to identify.

Many base and precious metal deposits fall into this category. The plumbing system for the hydrothermal solutions and reactivity of the host rock will control distribution of the intermediate temperature (mesothermal) mineralization. Mineralization will occur as disseminations, veins, and replacements.

Ore Minerals

Most sulphides have a metallic luster with the exception of sphalerite, realgar and orpiment. The most common sulphide mineral by far is pyrite.

PYRITE* — FeS_2. Brassy in color, not as yellow as chalcopyrite. Will not scratch with knife blade. Cubic and pyritohedron crystals.

See Simon and Schuster's *Rocks and Minerals,* mineral no. 31.
See Golden *Rocks and Minerals,* page 104.

CHALCOPYRITE* — $CuFeS_2$. Brassy yellow in color, brighter yellow than pyrite. Will show black scratch with knife blade.

See Simon and Schuster's *Rocks and Minerals,* mineral no. 18 (poor color).
See Golden *Rocks and Minerals,* page 98 (good yellow color on crystals at top right of page 99).

BORNITE* — Cu_5FeS_4. Iridescent "peacock" color.

See Simon and Schuster's *Rocks and Minerals,* mineral no. 14.
See Golden *Rocks and Minerals,* page 98.

ENARGITE — Cu_3AsS_4.

See Simon and Schuster's *Rocks and Minerals,* mineral no. 21.
See Golden *Rocks and Minerals,* page 116.

GALENA* — PbS. Lead gray; perfect cubic cleavage. Often found with silver and sphalerite.

> See Simon and Schuster's *Rocks and Minerals,* mineral no. 25.
> See Golden *Rocks and Minerals,* page 90.

SPHALERITE* — Zn(Fe)S. Submetallic resinous luster. Ruby sphalerite with little or no iron (Fe); the greater the percentage of iron, the blacker sphalerite gets. Often found with galena.

> See Simon and Schuster's *Rocks and Minerals,* mineral no. 17.
> See Golden *Rocks and Minerals,* page 96.

BISMUTHINITE — Bi_2S_3. Note long crystals like stibnite. Can have related green oxidation stain. Rare.

> See Simon and Schuster's *Rocks and Minerals,* mineral no. 29.
> See Golden *Rocks and Minerals,* page 86.

GOLD * — Au

> See Simon and Schuster's *Rocks and Minerals,* mineral no. 3.
> See Golden *Rocks and Minerals,* page 70.

ARSENOPYRITE* — FeAsS. Often associated with gold quartz veins; stains a dirty light yellow.

> See Simon and Schuster's *Rocks and Minerals,* mineral no. 35.
> See Golden *Rocks and Minerals,* page 106.

Gangue Minerals

* Minerals you should be able to identify.
In addition to quartz, gangue minerals include:

CALCITE * — $CaCO_3$. Rhombohedral cleavage, effervesces in acid.

> See Simon and Schuster's *Rocks and Minerals,* mineral no. 93.
> See Golden *Rocks and Minerals,* page 228.

DOLOMITE* — $CaMg(CO_3)_2$.

> See Simon and Schuster's *Rocks and Minerals,* mineral no. 94.
> See Golden *Rocks and Minerals,* page 230.

SIDERITE * — $FeCO_3$.

> See Simon and Schuster's *Rocks and Minerals,* mineral no. 91.

See Golden *Rocks and Minerals,* page 228.

BARITE* — BaSO$_4$. Note heavy specific gravity.

See Simon and Schuster's *Rocks and Minerals,* mineral no. 115.
See Golden *Rocks and Minerals,* page 240.

RHODOCHROSITE* — MnCO$_3$.

See Simon and Schuster's *Rocks and Minerals,* mineral no. 92.
See Golden *Rocks and Minerals,* page 230.

LOW TEMPERATURE MINERALS

As the hydrothermal solutions work their way farther from the heat source and nearer the surface, lower temperature (epithermal) mineralization occurs, either volcanic or nonvolcanic related. If the solutions come close to the surface, they may mix with ground water and may also break the surface as hot springs and fumaroles (see Figure 7-2). An idealized stratovolcanic model of mineralization is shown in Figure 7-3. Open space in veins, including crystal lined vugs, are indicative of near-surface epithermal mineralization. Minerals commonly epithermal are as follows:

FIGURE 7-2
Cross Section through an Epithermal Precious Metal Geothermal System
(Buchanan, 1981)

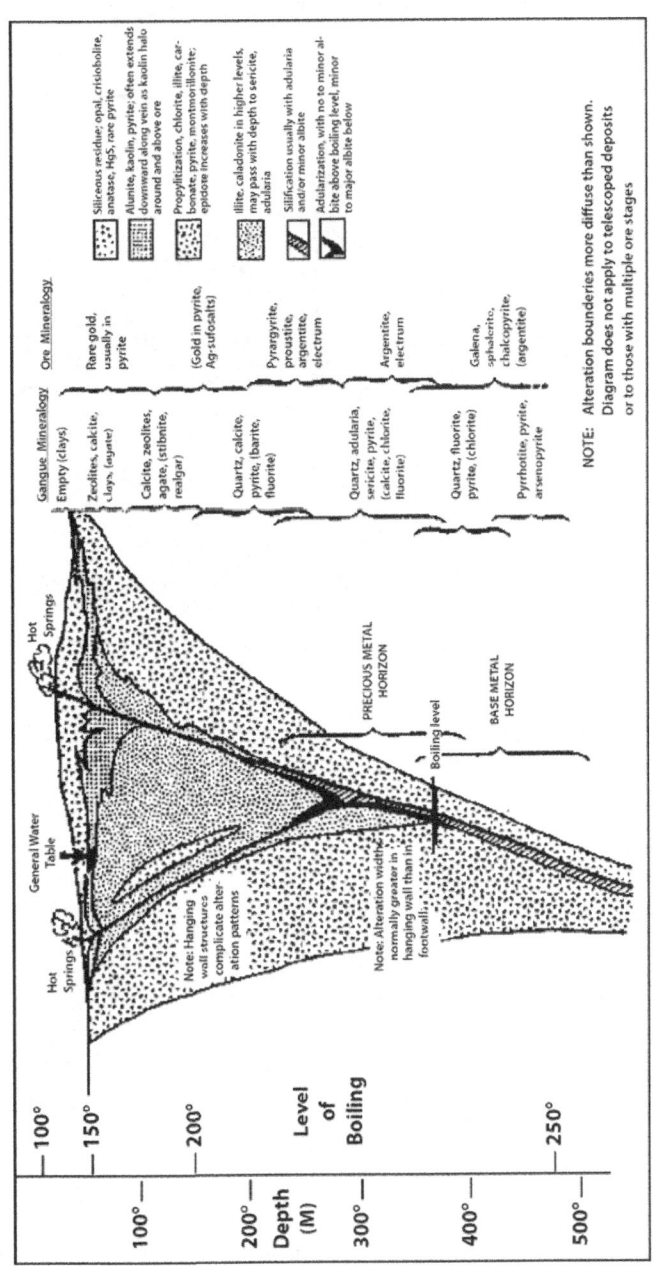

FIGURE 7-3
Idealized Model of Possible Ore Deposit Types
Related to a Stratovolcano
Modified After Sillitoe (1973)

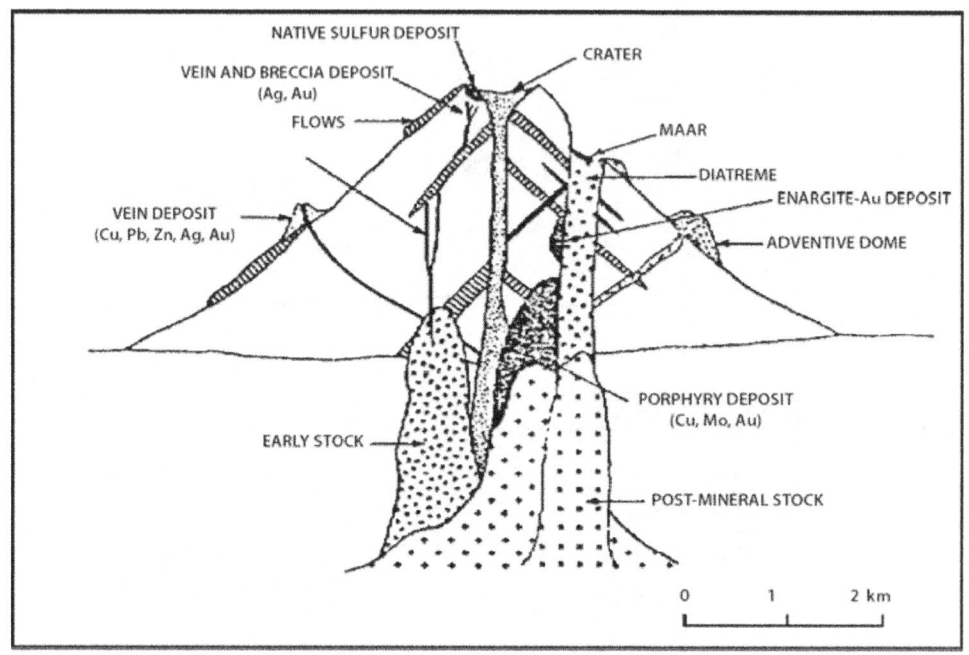

Ore Minerals

* Minerals you should be able to identify.

SULFUR* — S.
> See Simon and Schuster's *Rocks and Minerals,* mineral no. 12.
> See Golden *Rocks and Minerals,* page 78.

CINNABAR* — HgS. Distinctive red color, often in an opalite host rock.
> See Simon and Schuster's *Rocks and Minerals,* mineral no. 26.
> See Golden *Rocks and Minerals,* page 84.

ARGENTITE* — Ag_2S.
> See Simon and Schuster's *Rocks and Minerals,* mineral no. 15.
> See Golden *Rocks and Minerals,* page 92.

TETRAHEDRITE-TENNANTITE — $(Cu,Fe)_{12}(Sb,As)_4S_{13}$.
> See Simon and Schuster's *Rocks and Minerals,* mineral no. 19.
> See Golden *Rocks and Minerals,* page 114.

BARITE* — $BaSO_4$. Can form "blanket" deposits.
> See Simon and Schuster's *Rocks and Minerals,* mineral no. 115.
> See Golden *Rocks and Minerals,* page 240.

STIBNITE* — Sb_2S_3. Note elongated crystals.
> See Simon and Schuster's *Rocks and Minerals,* mineral no. 28.
> See Golden *Rocks and Minerals,* page 86.

MARCASITE* — FeS_2. Low temperature equivalent of pyrite. Note Cock's comb crystals.
> See Simon and Schuster's *Rocks and Minerals,* mineral no. 34.
> See Golden *Rocks and Minerals,* page 106.

REALGAR* — AsS. Distinctive red-orange color. Danger because of arsenic. (KEEP OUT OF REACH OF CHILDREN.)
> See Simon and Schuster's *Rocks and Minerals,* mineral no. 45.
> See Golden *Rocks and Minerals,* page 84.

ORPIMENT* — As_2S_3. Distinctive yellow color. Danger because of arsenic. (KEEP OUT OF REACH OF CHILDREN.)

See Simon and Schuster's *Rocks and Minerals,* mineral no. 46 (poor photograph).

See Golden *Rocks and Minerals,* page 84.

COPPER* — Cu.

See Simon and Schuster's *Rocks and Minerals,* mineral no. 1.

See Golden *Rocks and Minerals,* page 72.

SILVER* — Ag.

See Simon and Schuster's *Rocks and Minerals,* mineral no. 2.

See Golden *Rocks and Minerals,* page 72.

GOLD* — Au.

See Simon and Schuster's *Rocks and Minerals,* mineral no. 3.

See Golden *Rocks and Minerals,* page 70.

Gangue Minerals

Epithermal gangue minerals include quartz, calcite, dolomite and the following:

FLUORITE* — CaF_2. Greasy luster and colors of light green, blue, purple and white.

See Simon and Schuster's *Rocks and Minerals,* mineral no. 50.

See Golden *Rocks and Minerals,* page 124.

MANGANITE — MnO(OH).

See Simon and Schuster's *Rocks and Minerals,* mineral no. 86.

See Golden *Rocks and Minerals,* page 148.

TYPES OF HYDROTHERMAL DEPOSITS

Four general types of hydrothermal deposits occur, depending upon the chemistry of the magma, hydrothermal solutions, host rocks, temperature, pressure, and plumbing system.

1. Contact metamorphic zones and mineral deposits form through a process of metasomatic replacement of limestones and

dolomites by metal and silica ions. These ions are transported in gases and hydrothermal solutions originating from the magma.
See *Prospecting for Gemstones and Minerals,* pages 149 (bottom)-151.

2. Replacement mineral deposits occur where acid hydrothermal solutions come in contact with reactive country rock, such as limestone and dolomite. Many of the large deposits of lead, silver, zinc and barite are of this type.
See *Prospecting for Gemstones and Minerals,* pages 158-159.

3. Vein deposits occur when hydrothermal solutions encounter the right chemical, temperature and pressure conditions where minerals are deposited in the open spaces of the plumbing system itself.
See *Prospecting for Gemstones and Minerals,* pages 154-158.

4. Porphyry-Related Deposits.
See *Prospecting for Gemstones and Minerals,* page 156.

Because of the extremely complex nature of hydrothermal deposits, it is not uncommon to see evidence of overlapping of the four types of deposits discussed above, i.e., veins occurring in contact metamorphic zones and associated with replacement deposits, or veinlets in porphyry type deposits that are found cutting across contact metamorphic zones.

A fifth type of hydrothermal deposit is hybrid in nature and occurs when hydrothermal solutions mix with sea water (copper sulfide deposits of Cyprus), or ground water (low grade disseminated gold deposits of Nevada).

CONTACT METAMORPHIC DEPOSITS
During the later stages of emplacement, the upper parts of the magma may be intruded into overlaying sediments and volcanics. Residual hydrothermal solutions and volatiles are concentrating as "leftovers" and contain silica, sulphur, rare and precious metals and other elements and complexes.

During intrusion, the volatiles began reacting with the intruded country rock, resulting in the formation of the contact metamorphic zone. Limestone and dolomite are the most reactive rocks in the contact metamorphic zone and through the process of contact metasomatism, they can become calc silicates, skarns and tactites. The silicate nature of these rocks makes them brittle, and with additional intrusive pressure they can break and shatter, forming open space hosts for subsequent hydrothermal mineralization.

Development of the contact metamorphic zone depends upon the quantity of volatiles available to react with the country rock. Poorly developed contact zones may be only inches to a few feet wide, showing mainly baking and recrystallization. Well developed contact zones may be hundreds of feet wide, showing many of the metamorphic minerals listed in the Metamorphic Rock section herein.

During the contact metasomatism process, closely associated hydrothermal solutions may be active resulting in high temperature mineral deposits, either as disseminated mineralization or veinlets found in the tactite or skarn and adjacent granitic rock. Predominant contact metamorphic mineralization consists of molybdenum, iron and tungsten.

See Golden *Rocks and Minerals,* pages 82-83.

See *Prospecting for Gemstones and Minerals,* pages 149 (bottom)-151.

PORPHYRY-COPPER DEPOSITS

Most of the production of copper in the United States comes from large low-grade porphyry deposits mined from open pits. The term "porphyry" refers to the texture of the related intrusive igneous rock where large, well-formed feldspar crystals are set in a matrix of fine-grained crystals or glass. Recent ideas concerning the formation of many of the porphyry copper deposits suggests a close relationship to volcanic activity and crustal plate movement (see Figure 7-3).

Magma begins to cool and crystallize, as discussed in the Bowen's Reaction Series (see Figure 6-1). The prophyry texture of the intrusive suggests disturbance and emplacement to often very shallow depths of 3,000 to 4,000 feet. The emplaced magma may form magma chambers feeding volcanoes.

As emplacement occurs there is a related release in pressure, and the magma must rid itself of much of its internal water. This often happens explosively resulting in the shattering of the cooled outer shell of the intrusive and surrounding contact metamorphic zone and invaded country rock.

The hydrothermal solutions permeate through and chemically react with the shattered and broken host rock, finally mingling with ground water. Intense reaction in the shattered intrusive rock breaks down the orthoclase into the new minerals, sericite and quartz.

Kaolinite, a clay mineral, also forms from alteration of the feldspars. Where there is strong sericitic and kaolinitic alteration the rocks appear bleached, and in some cases, show iron staining.

Less intense chloritic alteration may develop in the outer fringes where the pyroxene and amphibole minerals are altered to the mineral chlorite, giving the rock a greenish tinge.

Mineralization consists of disseminations and veinlets of chalcopyrite, bornite, possibly gold, along with pyrite and quartz gangue. Porphyry deposits can be many millions of tons in size.

Source of the copper is thought to be both primary from the magma, and secondary from the surrounding rocks. Mineralization can be found in the intrusive and extending out into the intruded sedimentary and volcanic rocks, generally through the contact metamorphic zone.

See *Prospecting for Gemstones and Minerals,* page 156.

CHAPTER 8: Secondary Deposits

WEATHERING OF HYDROTHERMAL DEPOSITS

Hydrothermal mineral deposits consist predominately of primary sulphide mineralization and can form from near surface to depths of thousands of feet. Subsequent uplift and erosion over millions of years can strip off hundreds and thousands of feet of overlying rock, including upper parts of the mineralization, to where we see the present day surface exposures. A typical example could be Figure 8-1.

During weathering and erosion, many minerals in the host rocks and in the zone of mineralization are attacked chemically and dissolved. The more resistant minerals are generally not dissolved but are concentrated through mechanical processes, as discussed in Placer Deposits, herein.

FIGURE 8-1
Hypothetical Erosion of a Contact
Metamorphic Deposit

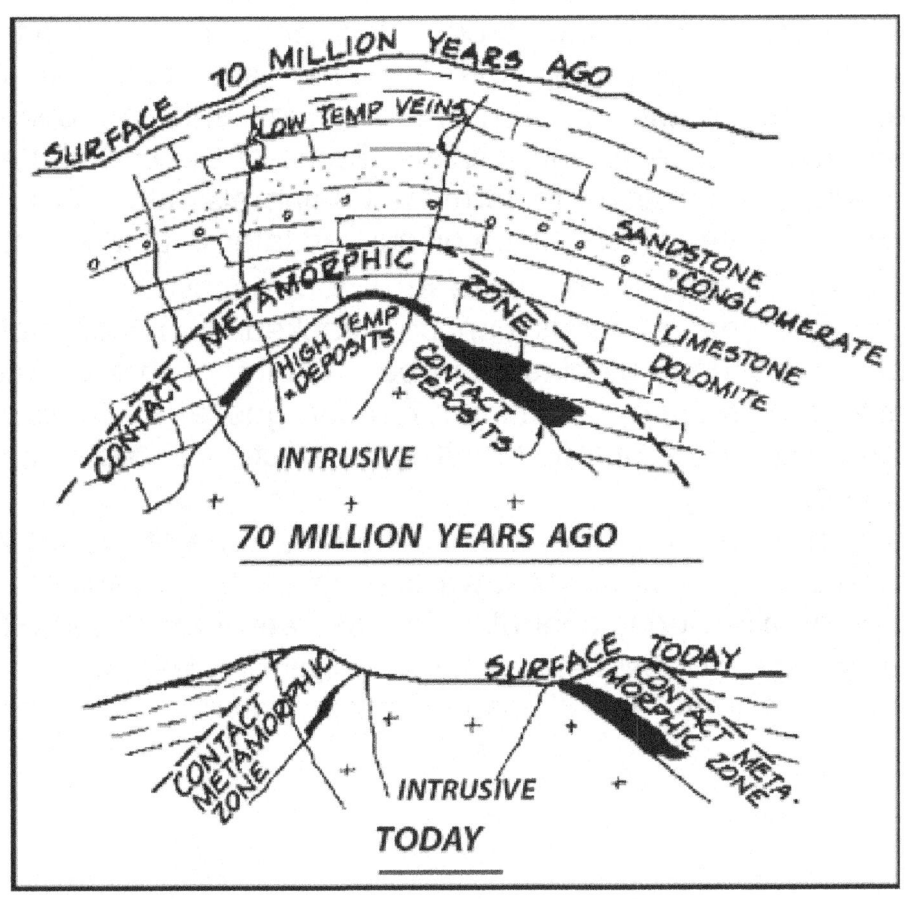

The principal agent is rain water which, combined with carbon dioxide picked up from the atmosphere, forms a weak acid. Once in the soil, the rain water can become strongly acidic if pyrite or marcasite is present, and is then able to attack other minerals.

The acid water percolating through limestone and dolomite can dissolve the rock, enlarging the fractures and then, at some distance, redeposit the calcium, magnesium and carbonate as calcite and dolomite veins and veinlets. Some of the carbonate may combine with other metals to form new minerals such as azurite, malachite or siderite, which will be discussed later in this section.

If the acid percolating waters are in a non-reactive rock, such as granite, the feldspar minerals can be attacked chemically forming kaolinite. Iron-bearing sulphides can be partially, or totally, oxidized to hematite and limonite, sometimes forming gossans. Gossans are the oxidized iron outcroppings that the prospectors of old sought out and explored.

The zone of reaction or leaching is called the zone of oxidation and is characterized by abundant brown and yellow iron staining. Depth of the zone of oxidation is controlled by the water table (Figure 8-2).

See *Prospecting for Gemstones and Minerals,* figure 74, page 164.

See Golden *Rocks and Minerals,* page 103 (top diagram).

FIGURE 8-2
Simplified Diagram of Oxidizing Sulphide Mineralization

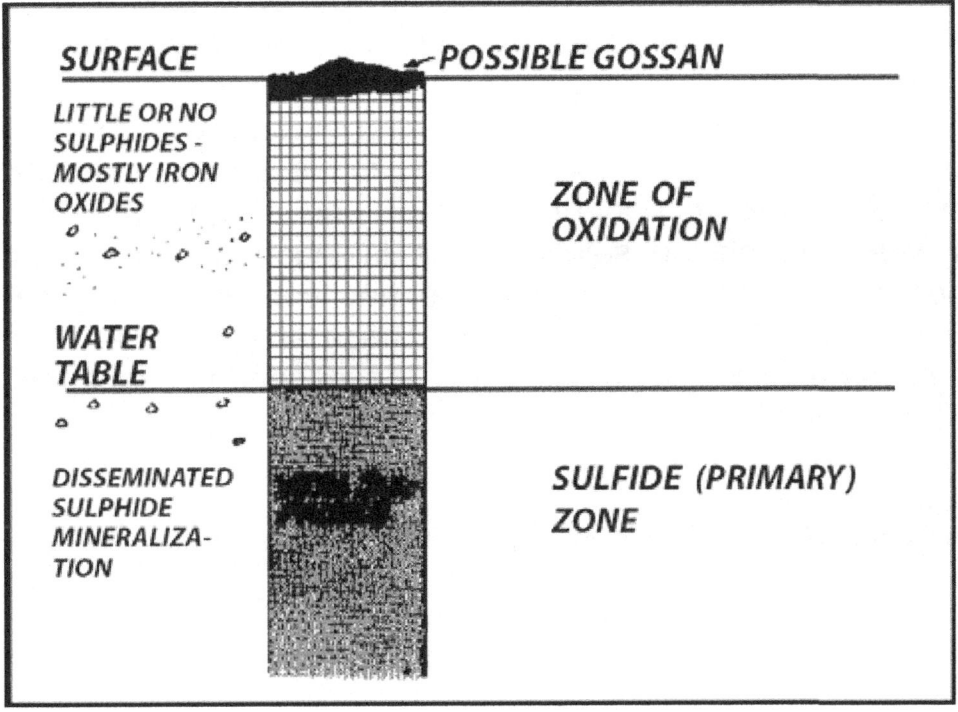

The zone of oxidation, or weathering, is best developed where there is a deep water table in arid or desert environments. Under certain conditions, oxide zones can be rapidly stripped off leaving mineralization exposed at the surface. This can occur where there has been recent landslides or in areas of glaciation.

Where there is much rainfall and a near surface water table, there will be little room for oxidation. Related to the zone of oxidation and water table is the secondary enriched zone. If the right conditions exist when percolating solutions rich in leached metals, such as copper or silver, reach the water table, new copper or silver minerals can form just below the water table. These are secondary minerals and the area of formation is called the secondary enriched zone (see Figure 8-3).

See *Prospecting for Gemstones and Minerals,* figure 74, page 164, and pages 205-208.

See Golden *Rocks and Minerals,* page 103 (top diagram).

FIGURE 8-3
Simplified Diagram of the Zone of Secondary Enrichment

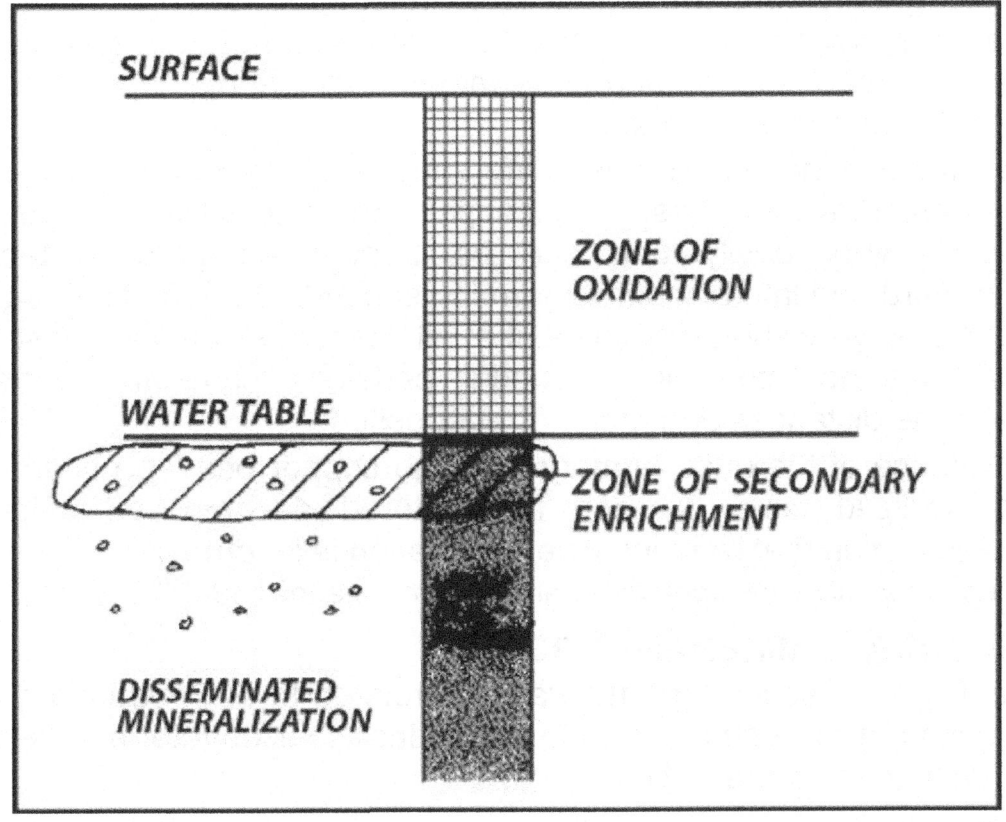

It should be pointed out that over thousands and millions of years of weathering and erosion, weather conditions and rainfall have varied greatly and the water table has fluctuated from deep to shallow many times. The water table today is not indicative of the water table in the past, and there may be several overlapping zones of oxidation and enrichment.

Sulphide minerals weather differently and the dissolved metals have different mobilities. Iron, copper, zinc and silver can go into solution very easily and can be transported great distances downward and laterally before forming secondary minerals. Lead will move only very short distances, if at all. Recent studies suggest that gold may go into solution, under certain circumstances, travel moderate distances and then be redeposited.

Evidence of the once primary iron and copper bearing minerals in the oxidized zone is seen in scattered decomposed sulphide mineralization that remains where oxidation is incomplete.

See *Prospecting for Gemstones and Minerals,* pages 159-168 (middle).

SECONDARY MINERALIZATION

The following secondary minerals are related to the weathering and oxidation of the primary copper sulphides: chalcopyrite, bornite and enargite (see Figure 8-4):

SECONDARY MINERALS

CHRYSOCOLLA* — $(Cu,Al)_2H_2Si_2O_5 \cdot nH_2O$. Can be confused with turquoise.

> See Simon and Schuster's *Rocks and Minerals,* mineral no. 242.
> See Golden *Rocks and Minerals,* page 180.

AZURITE* — $Cu_3(CO_3)_2(OH)_2$. Distinctive azure blue in color.

> See Simon and Schuster's *Rocks and Minerals,* mineral no. 99 (poor color in photo).
> See Golden *Rocks and Minerals,* page 234.

MALACHITE* — $Cu_2CO_3(OH)_2$. Distinctive green color.

> See Simon and Schuster's *Rocks and Minerals,* mineral no. 100.

See Golden *Rocks and Minerals,* pages 234 and 235.

TURQUOISE* — $CuAl_6(PO_4)(OH)_8•4H_2O$.

See Simon and Schuster's *Rocks and Minerals,* mineral no. 153.
See Golden *Rocks and Minerals,* page 244.

CUPRITE — Cu_2O.

See Simon and Schuster's *Rocks and Minerals,* page 55.
See Golden *Rocks and Minerals,* page 132.

COPPER (Native)* — Cu.

See Simon and Schuster's *Rocks and Minerals,* mineral no. 1.
See Golden *Rocks and Minerals,* page 72.

FIGURE 8-4
Ideal Cross Section of Anaconda Vein, Butte, Montana.
(From Emmons, W.H., *The Enrichment of Ore Deposits*, U.S. Geological Survey Bulletin 625, 1917)

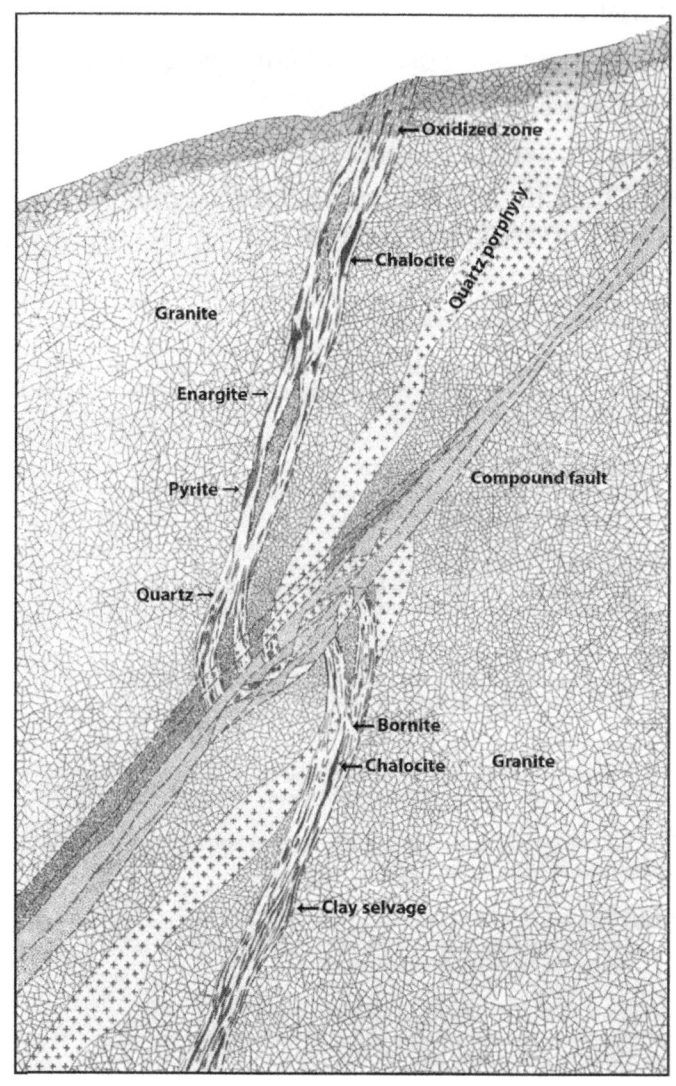

The following minerals are related to secondary enrichment from copper-bearing solutions:

CHALCOCITE* — Cu_2S. Sooty black.

See Simon and Schuster's *Rocks and Minerals,* mineral no. 13.
See Golden *Rocks and Minerals,* page 94.

COVELLITE* — CuS. Can look iridescent like bornite, but platy.

See Simon and Schuster's *Rocks and Minerals,* mineral no. 27.
See Golden *Rocks and Minerals,* page 102.

The following minerals are related to the weathering and oxidation of pyrite and other iron-bearing minerals:

LIMONITE* — $FeO(OH)$. Generally yellowish in color.

See Simon and Schuster's *Rocks and Minerals,* mineral no. 88.
See Golden *Rocks and Minerals,* page 150.

HEMATITE* — Fe_2O_3. Usually dark brown and massive. Red brown streak distinctive.

See Simon and Schuster's *Rocks and Minerals,* mineral no. 65.
See Golden *Rocks and Minerals,* page 136.

GOETHITE — $FeO(OH)$

See Simon and Schuster's *Rocks and Minerals,* mineral no. 85.
See Golden *Rocks and Minerals,* page 148.

The following minerals are associated with the weathering and oxidation of galena (PbS). Cerussite and anglesite will form very close to where the galena existed:

CERUSSITE* — $PbCO_3$.

See Simon and Schuster's *Rocks and Minerals,* mineral no. 98.
See Golden *Rocks and Minerals,* page 232.

ANGLESITE * — $PbSO_4$.

See Simon and Schuster's *Rocks and Minerals,* mineral no. 116.
See Golden *Rocks and Minerals,* page 240.

PYROMORPHITE — $Pb_5(PO_4)_3Cl$.

See Simon and Schuster's *Rocks and Minerals,* mineral no. 141.
See Golden *Rocks and Minerals,* page 250.

VANADINITE — $Pb_5(VO_4)_3Cl$.

See Simon and Schuster's *Rocks and Minerals,* mineral no. 143.
See Simon and Schuster's *Rocks and Minerals,* page 250.

The following minerals are associated with the weathering and oxidation of sphalerite (ZnS):

SMITHSONITE* — $ZnCO_3$.

See Simon and Schuster's *Rocks and Minerals,* mineral no. 90.
See Golden *Rocks and Minerals,* page 230.

HEMIMORPHITE — $Zn_4Si_2 O_7(OH)_2 \cdot H_2O$.

See Simon and Schuster's *Rocks and Minerals,* mineral no. 179,
See Golden *Rocks and Minerals,* page 230.

The following minerals are related to the secondary enrichment of silver:

CERARGYRITE — AgCl. (Horn silver).

See Golden *Rocks and Minerals,* page 122.

PYRARGYRITE — Ag_3SbS_3. (Ruby silver).

See Simon and Schuster's *Rocks and Minerals,* mineral no. 40.
See Golden *Rocks and Minerals,* page 112.

PROUSTITE — Ag_3AsS_3. (Ruby silver).

See Simon and Schuster's *Rocks and Minerals,* mineral no. 39.
See Golden *Rocks and Minerals,* page 112.

The following minerals are associated with the weathering and oxidation of manganese bearing minerals:

PYROLUSITE — MnO_2.

See Simon and Schuster's *Rocks and Minerals,* mineral no. 73.
See Golden *Rocks and Minerals,* page 144.

PSILOMELANE — $BaMnMn_8O_{16}(OH)_4$.

See Simon and Schuster's *Rocks and Minerals,* mineral no. 74.
See Golden *Rocks and Minerals,* page 150.

Gangue Minerals

See *Prospecting for Gemstones and Minerals,* page 168 (top).

DEPOSITS RELATED TO CIRCULATING GROUND WATER

Ground water can become enriched in silica, carbonate, uranium and other ions after traveling through certain rock types or co-mingling with hydrothermal solutions. Deposits of silica minerals, carbonate minerals, uranium bearing minerals and others can form most commonly in sedimentary and volcanic rocks, but also in metamorphic and intrusive igneous rocks, sometimes related to hot springs and fumeroles. The porosity and fracturing found in these rocks control the shape and size of the deposits.

See *Prospecting for Gemstones and Minerals,* pages 210-222.

SILICA MINERALS

The silica minerals are a group of minerals with the formula SiO_2.

CRYSTALLINE SILICA MINERALS

— crystals can be seen with the eye.

QUARTZ — SiO_2. Varieties include:

MILKY QUARTZ — with inclusions of CO and H_2O.

SMOKY QUARTZ.

AMETHYST QUARTZ — with impurities of Fe.

ROSE QUARTZ — with impurities of Ti or Mn.

SAGENITE — with inclusions of other minerals such as rutile.

CITRINE — with impurities of Fe.

See Simon and Schuster's *Rocks and Minerals,* mineral no. 244.
See Golden *Rocks and Minerals,* pages 206-207.

CRYPTOCRYSTALLINE SILICA MINERALS
— crystals not visible to the eye.

CHALCEDONY — SiO_2 — translucent, no banding. Varieties include:

AGATE — if banding or inclusions.

ONYX — straight banding.

TIGER EYE — yellow brown, appears fibrous.

CHERT — SiO_2 — Opaque, light will not travel into mineral. Generally shades of gray. Varieties include:

FLINT — Black.

JASPER — Red, brown, orange or green.
> See Simon and Schuster's *Rocks and Minerals,* mineral no. 245.
> See Golden *Rocks and Minerals,* pages 208-209.

AMPHOROUS SILICA
— Non-crystalline with included water in the crystal structure.

OPAL — Greasy luster; Hardness 5.5-6.5.
> See Simon and Schuster's *Rocks and Minerals,* mineral no. 248.
> See Golden *Rocks and Minerals,* pages 210-211.

Different silica minerals may occur together. For example, a geode may contain chalcedony, banded agate and opal, along with crystalline quartz.
> See Simon and Schuster's *Rocks and Minerals,* mineral no. 245. The bottom
> photograph of the geode from Brazil shows outer bands of agate with
> quartz crystals in the center.

Petrified wood commonly consists of chert, jasper, chalcedony, agate and opal, typically showing beautifully preserved wood grain.

CARBONATE MINERALS
Carbonate minerals can fill fractures and form deposits related to circulating ground water, commonly in areas of limestone and

dolomites.

CALCITE — $CaCO_3$.

See Simon and Schuster's *Rocks and Minerals,* mineral no. 93.
See Golden *Rocks and Minerals,* page 228.

ARAGONITE — $CaCO_3$.

See Simon and Schuster's *Rocks and Minerals,* mineral no. 95.
See Golden *Rocks and Minerals,* page 232.

CALICHE — A calcium carbonate with impurities; crust on near-surface rock fractures. Found in arid to semi-arid areas. Formed from the evaporation of rain water.

URANIUM MINERALS

Uranium bearing minerals can be deposited from ground water coming in contact with organic material, such as wood in conglomerates and sandstone.

CARNOTITE — $K_2(UO_2)_2(VO_4)_2 \cdot nH_2O$. Canary yellow.

See Simon and Schuster's *Rocks and Minerals,* mineral no. 156.
See Golden *Rocks and Minerals,* pages 248-249.
See *Prospecting for Gemstones and Minerals,* pages 228 (bottom) -230.

ZEOLITE MINERALS

A group of 22 minerals, called zeolites, can be commonly found lining vesicles (cavities) in basalts and other volcanics, lake sediments and other host rocks, along with silica minerals and carbonates. Common zeolite minerals are:

NATROLITE — $Na_2(Al_2Si_3)O_{10} \cdot 2H_2O$.

See Simon and Schuster's *Rocks and Minerals,* mineral no. 266.

HEULANDITE — $(Na,Ca)_{4-6}Al_6(Al,Si)_4Si_{26}O_{72} \cdot 24H_2O$.

See Simon and Schuster's *Rocks and Minerals,* mineral no. 270.
See Golden *Rocks and Minerals,* pages 226-227.

STILBITE — $NaCa_2(Al_5Si1_3)O_{36} \cdot 14H_2O$.

See Simon and Schuster's *Rocks and Minerals,* mineral no. 271.
See Golden *Rocks and Minerals,* pages 226-227.

CHABAZITE — $Ca(Al_2Si_4)O_{12} \cdot 6H_2O$.

See Simon and Schuster's *Rocks and Minerals,* mineral no. 274.
See Golden *Rocks and Minerals,* pages 226-227.

MINERALS ASSOCIATED WITH ZEOLITE MINERALS

ANALCITE (ANALCIME)—$NaAlSi_2 \cdot O_6H_2O$.

See Simon and Schuster's *Rocks and Minerals,* mineral no. 251.
See Golden *Rocks and Minerals,* page 224.

PREHNITE — $Ca_2Al_2Si_3O_{10}(OH)_2$.

See Simon and Schuster's *Rocks and Minerals,* mineral no. 220.
See Golden *Rocks and Minerals,* page 196.

RESIDUAL DEPOSITS

The weathering of certain rocks can result in the formation of economic residual deposits of clay, aluminum, nickel and iron.

MONTMORILLONITE (BENTONITE) —
$(Na,Ca)_{0.33}(Al,Mg)_2Si_4(OH)_2 \cdot nH_2O$. Swelling clay deposits.

See Simon and Schuster's *Rocks and Minerals,* mineral no. 234.
See Golden *Rocks and Minerals,* page 200.

BAUXITE — Al_2O_3OH. An important ore of aluminum; forms from the weathering of alumina-rich igneous rocks in subtropical climates.

See Simon and Schuster's *Rocks and Minerals,* mineral no. 83.
See Golden *Rocks and Minerals,* page 148.

NICKEL — Nickel-bearing laterites form from the weathering of nickel-rich igneous rocks in subtropical climates.

SEPIOLITE — $Mg_9Si_{12}O_{30}(OH)_6 \cdot 10H_2O$. A surface alteration product of magnesite and serpentine.

See Simon and Schuster's *Rocks and Minerals,* mineral no. 243.
See Golden *Rocks and Minerals,* page 202.

CHAPTER 9:
Placer Deposits

INTRODUCTION

The erosion of weathered rocks and minerals results in the mechanical concentration of the more resistant higher specific gravity minerals. When the right conditions exist, valuable minerals concentrate to form placer deposits.

Placers are classified according to the way they are formed. Mechanical concentration starts where the rocks and minerals are exposed at the surface. Little by little, the vein or rock is broken down, forming soils and related concentrations of valuable minerals (residual placers). Gravity, rain and snow aid in the movement of the soil downslope with a further concentration of the valuable minerals (eluvial placers).

As the soils enter stream channels, water plays a more important part in the continued concentration of the valuable minerals (stream placers, glacial stream placers and bajada placers). The ordinary stream placer is by far the most important.

Concentration of valuable minerals can also be accomplished by wind (eolian placers) and by wave action along coastlines (beach placers).

See *Prospecting for Gemstones and Minerals,* pages 169-173; figure 75, page 169; and figure 78, page 172.

Placer Mining with a Cradle Rocker

CLASSIFICATION OF PLACER DEPOSITS
Residual Placers
Long, continued weathering of mineralized veins and surface rocks breaks down the mineral constituents. The resistant minerals will collect near the outcrop while the softer and less resistant minerals are carried away by erosion. See Figure 9-1 A.

Eluvial Placers
Residual placers on a hillside will slowly begin to "creep" down slope into rivulets and gulleys toward the nearest stream channel. Concentrations of valuable minerals along the hillside, downslope from the outcrop are eluvial placers. See Figure 9-1 A & B.

Stream Placers
Stream placers consist of valuable minerals concentrated in sand and gravel sorted by the action of running water. Placers formed in recent time will occupy the active stream channel. If formed in ancient times, the placer deposits may occupy benches elevated above the present day channel. See Figure 9-1 A, 9-1 B and 9-2.

FIGURE 9-1
Sketch Map and Cross-Section
Showing Development of Gold Placer Deposits
(After Jenkins: California Division Of Mines
Special Publication 340)

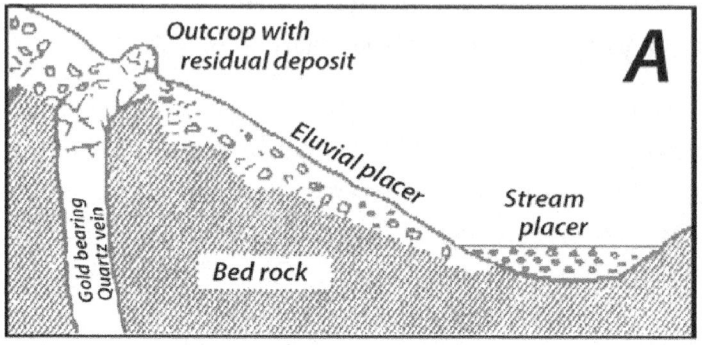

Diagram Showing Development of
Eluvial and Stream Placers.

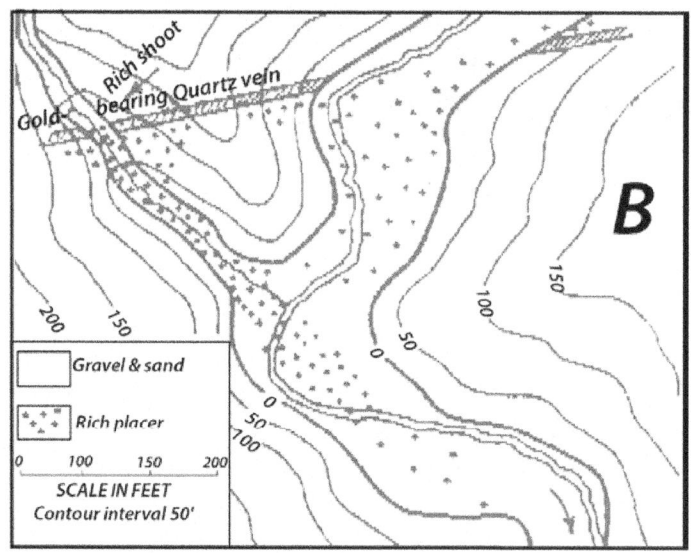

Sketch Map Showing the
Development of Rich Placers.

FIGURE 9-2
Typical Sites for Stream Placer Accumulations
(From Skinner, 1969)

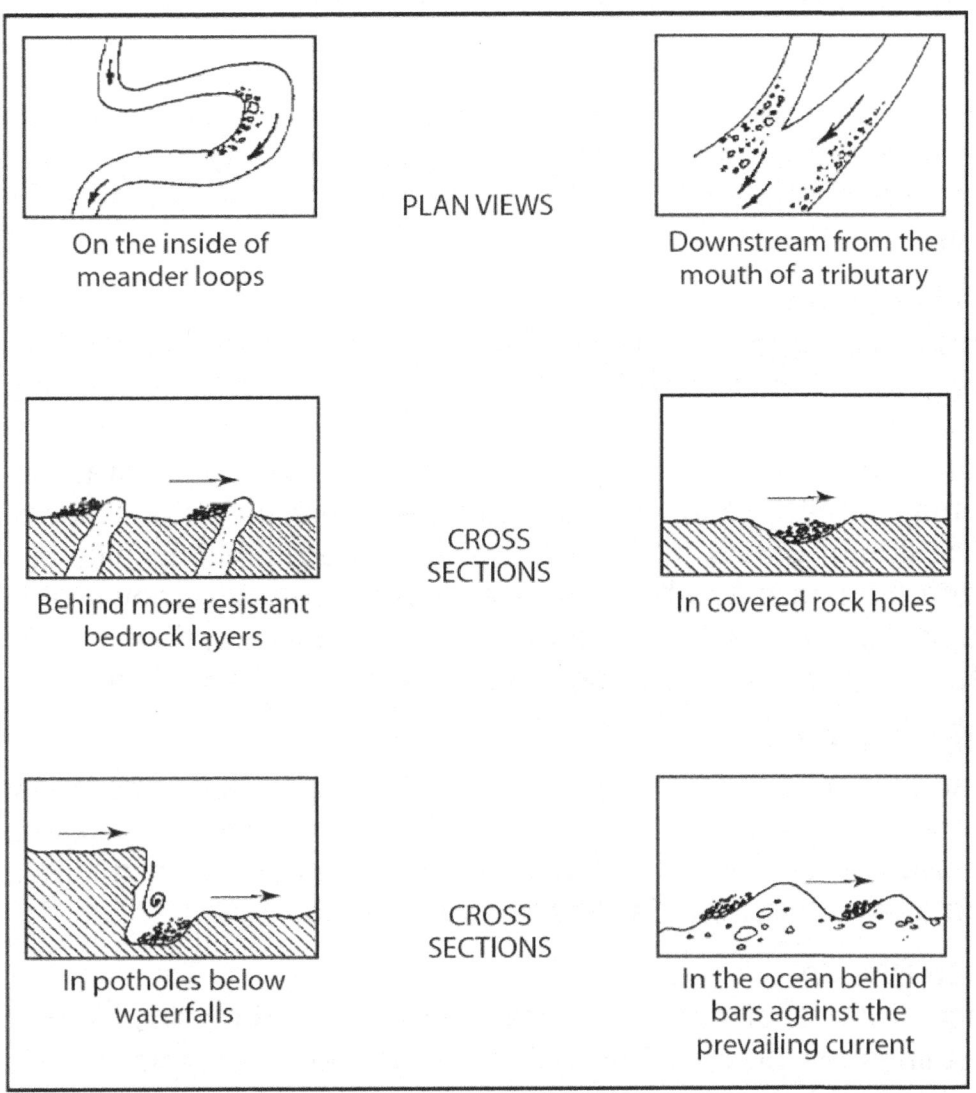

PLAN VIEWS

On the inside of
meander loops

Downstream from the
mouth of a tributary

CROSS
SECTIONS

Behind more resistant
bedrock layers

In covered rock holes

CROSS
SECTIONS

In potholes below
waterfalls

In the ocean behind
bars against the
prevailing current

Obstructing or deflecting barriers allow faster-moving waters to carry away the suspended load of light and fine-grained materials while trapping the more dense and coarse particles, which are moving along the bottom by rolling or by partial suspension.

Glacial-Stream Placers
Glaciers do not concentrate minerals into placer deposits. The waters derived from the melting glacial ice may be sufficient to cause concentration of valuable minerals downstream from the glacier.

Bajada Placers
Bajada placers form in arid climates and are related to alluvial fans. Alluvial fans form at the base of a mountain range as the result of flash flood erosion and transportation of rock and mineral material. When the waters emerge from narrow canyons draining the mountain range, there is a sudden decrease in water velocity and the boulders, gravel and sand are deposited, building alluvial fans. Bajada placers may show surface enrichment by removal of lighter material by wind and sheet floods. Placer concentrations are usually erratic because of the wandering nature of the channelways.

Eolian Placers
Eolian placers are formed by wind action. Sand dunes composed of the mineral gypsum are found in Utah and represent an example of an eolian placer. Wind action can also remove large quantities of fine material enriching desert residual placers.

Beach Placers
Concentrations of heavy minerals occur in various locations along coast lines as the result of the action of shore currents and waves. Materials broken down from sea cliffs or washed into the sea by streams are sorted and distributed by size and specific gravity.

Beach placers can be found along present beaches or elevated in ancient beach sands. The beach placers of economic importance are those that have been reconcentrated over and over again.

GOLD PLACERS

Gold, because of its value, is the most sought-after placer mineral. Gold is also a "natural" for placer concentration because of its high specific gravity (19+) and durability and can be found in all of the previously described types of deposits.

The great majority of gold placers have been derived from the weathering and disintegration of gold-bearing veins, shear zones, replacement deposits or the reworking of older gold placers.

Volumes have been written about placer gold and numerous books are available which discuss gold placer deposits and placer mining methods. Nearly every western state Bureau or Division of Mines has published reports about placer gold.

GOLD — Au

See Simon and Schuster's *Rocks and Minerals,* mineral no. 3.

See Golden *Rocks and Minerals,* page 70.

The following minerals may be associated with placer gold: magnetite (black sand), pyrite, silver.

OTHER PLACERS

The source of placer minerals lies in the rocks found in the area of the stream drainage. If you know the geology (rock types and mineralization) within the area of the stream drainage you can predict placer deposits you might expect to find.

Streams cutting belts of serpentine and related ultramafic rocks may yield chromite, diamond, olivine and platinum placer deposits.

Contact and regional metamorphic rocks within the area of the stream drainage may yield corundum, garnet, ilmenite, magnetite and scheelite placer deposits.

Mineralized granite and pegmatites can yield placer deposits of cassiterite, corundum, quartz crystals, topaz, zircon, and the below listed minerals:

COLUMBITE-TANTALITE — $(Fe,Mn)(Nb,Ta)_2O_6$

See Simon and Schuster's *Rocks and Minerals,* mineral no. 77.

MONAZITE — $(Ce,La,Nd,Th)PO_4$, Rare earth

See Simon and Schuster's *Rocks and Minerals,* mineral no. 130.
See Golden *Rocks and Minerals, page 246.*

RUTILE — TiO_2

See Simon and Schuster's *Rocks and Minerals,* mineral no. 71.
See Golden *Rocks and Minerals,* page 142.

WOLFRAMITE — $(Fe,Mn)WO_4$

See Golden *Rocks and Minerals,* page 254.

CHAPTER 10: Gemstones

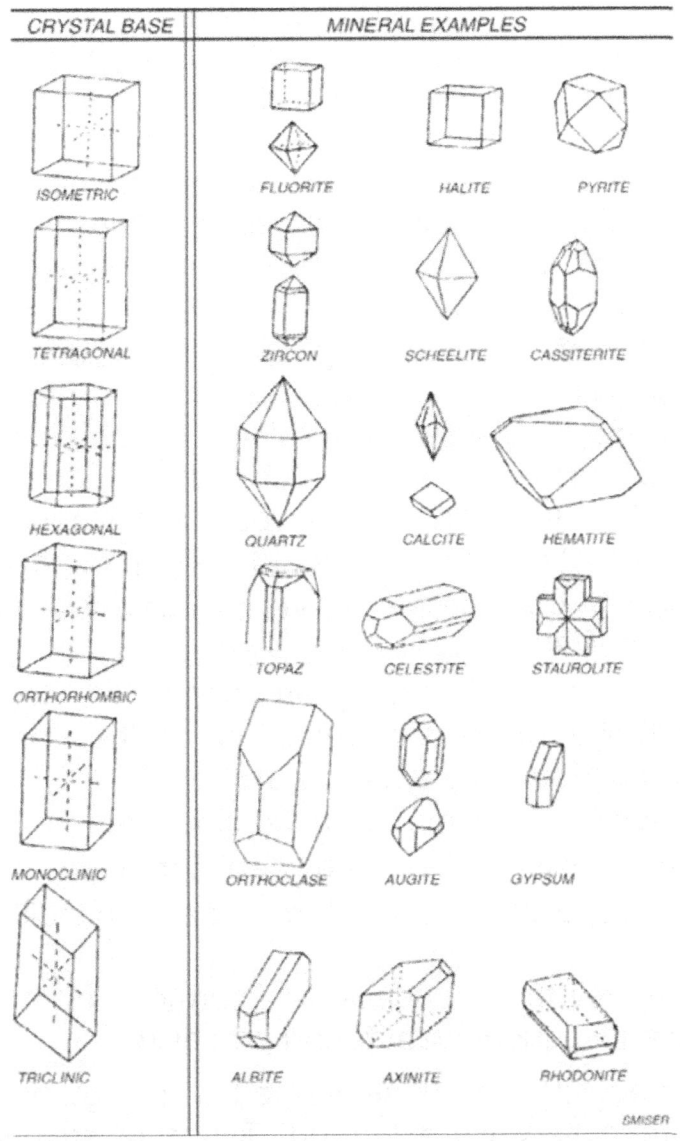

Six of the seven crystal systems and mineral examples.
(From Field, R.M., *Geology – College Outline Series,*
Barnes & Noble, Inc., 1951)

INTRODUCTION

Gemstones have held a special place in the history of man. Because of their rarity, appearance and aura of mystery they were held and shown as an expression of wealth and status. Gemstones were also used as medicine against illness and as having supernatural powers, which led to assigning birthstones to the divisions of the zodiac. Today, the precious gemstone is often viewed as only a capital investment, while the semi-precious gemstone is used in everyday jewelry.

Some of the fun of "rockhounding" is the anticipation of finding and the actual discovery of gemstones. It should be apparent now that gemstones are found in specific geologic environments. The ability to locate the geologic environment that might yield certain gemstones in the field will narrow your target zone considerably, saving you time and money and should make prospecting more fun.

See *Prospecting for Gemstones and Minerals,* pages 333-346.
See *Gemstones of the World,* page 8.

Gemstones are found in primary and secondary deposits. Primary deposits are those where the gems are in their original place of formation. Types of primary deposits are:

magmatic deposits — formed from cooling magma;

sedimentary deposits — formed by sedimentation;

metamorphic deposits — formed from the recrystallization of other rocks; and

hydrothermal related deposits — formed from hydrothermal solutions and subsequent weathering processes.

Secondary deposits are those formed where gems are in places other than where they were formed. Types of secondary deposits are:

placer (alluvial deposits) — formed by river or stream waters;

marine deposits — formed by ocean wave action; and

aeolian deposits — formed by wind action.

The yield from primary deposits is usually small because of the volume of rock that must be handled. Placer yields are usually greater because nature has aided in the concentrating of the gems.

See *Gemstones of the World,* pages 49-51.

IMPORTANT PRECIOUS AND SEMIPRECIOUS GEMSTONES

The following precious and semiprecious gemstones, including varieties, are listed in alphabetical order:

• BERYL — $Be_3Al_2Si_6O_{18}$. Hardness 7.5-8.

Varieties include:

Aquamarine — blue green

See *Gemstones of the World*, page 94.

Emerald — green

See *Gemstones of the World*, page 90.

Golden Beryl — golden yellow

Goshemite — colorless

Helidor — yellow and brown

Morganite — pink to red

These commonly occur in complex pegmatites. Less commonly occur in medium to high grade regional metamorphic environments in silica-poor schists and marbles. Also found in placers related to the above deposits.

See Simon and Schuster's *Rocks and Minerals,* mineral no. 188.
See Golden *Rocks and Minerals,* page 172.
See *Gemstones of the World,* page 96.

• CHRYSOBERYL — $BeAl_2O_4$. Hardness 8.5.

Varieties include:

Alexandrite — emerald green

Cat's Eye — honey yellow

These occur in complex pegmatites. Less commonly found in medium grade metamorphic environments in mica schists and marbles. Also found in placers related to the above deposits.

See Simon and Schuster's *Rocks and Minerals,* mineral no. 62.

See Golden *Rocks and Minerals,* page 146.
See *Gemstones of the World,* page 98.

• CORUNDUM — Al_2O_3. Hardness 9.

Varieties include:

Padparadschah — Orange

Ruby — Red

See *Gemstones of the World*, page 82

Sapphire — All other colors of gem quality corundum

See *Gemstones of the World,* page 86.

These occur in silica poor intrusive igneous rocks (syenites and syenite pegmatites), marbles and hornfels in contact metamorphic environments and mica schists in high grade regional metamorphic environments. Also found in placers related to the above deposits.

See Simon and Schuster's *Rocks and Minerals,* mineral no. 64.
See Golden *Rocks and Minerals,* page 134.

• DIAMOND — C. Colorless, yellow, brown, gray, green, black. Hardness 10.

Occurs in kimberlite (altered peridotite) pipes. Also found in related placer deposits.

See Simon and Schuster's *Rocks and Minerals,* mineral no. 11.
See Golden *Rocks and Minerals,* page 76.
See *Gemstones of the World,* pages 70-81.

• FELDSPAR — $KAlSi_3O_8$ and $(Na, Ca) AlSi_3O_8$. Hardness 6.

See *Gemstones of the World*, pages 164-167.

Varieties include:

Amazonite (microcline) — light bluish green

Occurs in pegmatites.

See Simon and Schuster's *Rocks and Minerals,* mineral no. 255.
See Golden *Rocks and Minerals,* page 214.

Labradorite — blues and greens

Occurs in intrusive and extrusive igneous rocks.

See Simon and Schuster's *Rocks and Minerals,* mineral no. 259.
See Golden *Rocks and Minerals,* page 221.

Moonstone (orthoclase and albite) — light yellow

Occurs in porphyritic igneous rocks and pegmatites.

See Simon and Schuster's *Rocks and Minerals,* mineral no. 256.
See Golden *Rocks and Minerals,* pages 216-219.

Sunstone (oligoclase) — light yellow

See Simon and Schuster's *Rocks and Minerals,* mineral no. 259.
See Golden *Rocks and Minerals,* page 218.

• GARNET — A group of six minerals listed below:

See Golden *Rocks and Minerals,* pages 162-163.
See *Gemstones of the World,* pages 104-107.

SPESSARTITE — $Mn_3Al2Si_3O_{12}$. Shades of red. Hardness 7.3.

Occurs in complex pegmatites and in schists in regional metamorphic environments.

PYROPE — $Mg_3Al_2Si_3O_{12}$. Deep red to reddish black. Hardness 7.5.

Rhodolite — pale purple variety

Occurs in peridotites and serpentinized peridotites. Also found in placers related to the above deposits.

See Simon and Schuster's *Rocks and Minerals,* mineral no. 160.

ALMANDINE (ALMANDITE) — $Fe_3Al_2Si_3O_{12}$. Red, brown and brownish black. Hardness 7.5.

Occurs in hornfels in contact metamorphic environments, schists in medium grade regional metamorphic environments, and in some intrusive diorite rocks. Also found in placers related to the above deposits.

See Simon and Schuster's *Rocks and Minerals,* mineral no. 161.

GROSSULAR (GROSSULARITE) — $Ca_3Al_2Si_3O_{12}$. Colorless, white, yellow, pink, green, brown. Hardness 7.3.

Occurs in hornfels in contact metamorphic environments.

See Simon and Schuster's *Rocks and Minerals,* mineral no. 162.

UVAROVITE — $Ca_3Cr_2Si_3O_{12}$. Emerald green. Hardness 7.5.
Occurs in chromite-rich peridotites and serpentines.
See Simon and Schuster's *Rocks and Minerals,* mineral no. 163.

ANDRADITE — $Ca_3Fe_2^{+3}Si_3O_{12}$. Many colors. Hardness 6.1-6.5.
Varieties include:
  Demantoid — green
  Topazolite — yellow
  Melanite — brown and black
These occur in pegmatites and hornfels and skarns in contact metamorphic environments.
See Simon and Schuster's *Rocks and Minerals,* mineral no. 164.

• JADEITE — $Na(Al,Fe^{+3})Si_2O_6$. Colorless, shades of green, black (darker as Fe^{+3} content increases). Hardness 6.5-7.
Occurs in blue schists in low grade metamorphic environments. Also occurs in serpentinized silica deficient ultramafic rocks.
See Simon and Schuster's *Rocks and Minerals,* mineral no. 196.
See Golden *Rocks and Minerals,* page 180.
See *Gemstones of the World,* page 154.

• LAZURITE — $(Na,Ca)_8(Al,Si)_{12}O_{24}(S,SO_4)$. Blue and green with violet tints. Hardness 5-5.5.
Lapis Lazuli — green variety
Occurs with calcite, diopside and pyrite in hornfels in contact metamorphic environments.
See Simon and Schuster's *Rocks and Minerals,* mineral no. 264.
See Golden *Rocks and Minerals,* page 224.
See *Gemstones of the World,* page 172.

• NEPHRITE — $Ca_2(Mg,Fe)_5Si_8O_{22}(OH)_2$ (variety of actinolite). White, green, gray, brown and lavender. Hardness 6-6.2. More common type of jade than jadeite.
Occurs in mafic schists in medium grade regional metamorphic environments.

See Simon and Schuster's *Rocks and Minerals,* mineral no. 205.
See Golden *Rocks and Minerals,* page 182.
See *Gemstones of the World,* page 156.

• OPAL — $SiO_2 \cdot nH_2O$. Various colors. Hardness 5.5-6.5.

Black Opal — black, dark blue and green with fine play of colors
Fire Opal — orange-yellow to red with play of colors
White Opal — white or bright body color with fine play of colors
Commonly precipitated from silica-rich hot springs and ground water in volcanic and sedimentary rocks in fractures and cavities.
See Simon and Schuster's *Rocks and Minerals,* mineral no. 248.
See Golden *Rocks and Minerals,* page 210.
See *Gemstones of the World,* pages 150-153.

• PERIDOT — Mg_2SiO_4. Light green. Hardness 6.5-7 (variety of fosterite, which is in the olivine group of minerals).
See Simon and Schuster's *Rocks and Minerals,* mineral no. 159.
See Golden *Rocks and Minerals,* page 164.
See *Gemstones of the World,* page 158.

• QUARTZ — SiO_2. Colorless, milky and various colors. Hardness 7.
Varieties include:
Rock Crystal — colorless
Amethyst — purple to violet, because of Fe impurities
Citrine — yellow to orange, because of Fe impurities
Rose Quartz — pink, because of Ti or Mn impurities
Smoky Quartz — dark brown to black
Sagenite — with rodlike or hairlike inclusions of rutile or tourmaline
Adventurine — with spangled inclusions of mica or hematite
Tiger's Eye — Yellow brown fiberous replacement of crysotile (asbestos)
These occur in pegmatites and as veins in igneous, sedimentary and metamorphic environments and related placers.
See Simon and Schuster's *Rocks and Minerals,* mineral no. 244.
See Golden *Rocks and Minerals,* pages 206, 210,

See *Gemstones of the World,* pages 116-125.

• CHALCEDONY — SiO_2. Many colors.

Varieties include:

Agate — banded variegated

Fire Agate — play of colors

Moss Agate — moss-like inclusions

Onyx — straight banding

Bloodstone (heliotrope) — dark green, spotted with red inclusions

Chrysoprase — apple green

Carnelian — red, orange-red, to reddish brown

Sard — red to reddish brown

Sardonyx — sard and carnelian in layers

Jasper — red, yellow, brown and green

These occur commonly as a low temperature precipitate from silca-rich ground water in igneous, sedimentary, and metamorphic environments. Also occur in placers related to the above deposits.

See Simon and Schuster's *Rocks and Minerals,* mineral no. 245.

See Golden *Rocks and Minerals,* page 208.

See *Gemstones of the World,* pages 126-147.

• SPINEL — $MgAl_2O_4$. Colorless, red, yellow, blue, green. Hardness 8.

Varieties include:

Almandine Spinel — purple

Pleonast — blue, dark green to black

Rubicelle — red, pink, rose, yellow to orange

These occur at high temperature in silica-poor igneous rocks, contact metamorphic, and high grade regional metamorphic environments. Also occur in related alluvial and marine placers.

See Simon and Schuster's *Rocks and Minerals,* mineral no. 57.

See Golden *Rocks and Minerals,* page 138.

See *Gemstones of the World,* page 100.

• TOPAZ — $Al_2SiO_4(F,OH)_2$. Colorless, yellow, blue, green, violet. Hardness 8.

Occurs at high temperature in complex pegmatites and in miarolitic cavities in rhyolites. Also occurs in related placer deposits.

See Simon and Schuster's *Rocks and Minerals,* mineral no. 169.
See Golden *Rocks and Minerals,* page 166.
See *Gemstones of the World,* page 102.

• TOURMALINE — $(Na,Ca)(Mg,Fe,Al,Mn,Li)_3Al_6(BO_3)_3(Si_6O_{18})(OH,F)_4$. Hardness 7-7.5.

Varieties include:
Achroite — colorless
Dravite (NaMg rich) — dark orange brown
Elbaite (NaLiAl rich) — green, pink, watermelon
Indicolite — blue
Rubellite (siberite) — red to purple
Schorl (NaFe rich) — black
Verdelite — green
These occur in complex pegmatites and related placers.

See Simon and Schuster's *Rocks and Minerals,* mineral no. 190.
See Golden *Rocks and Minerals,* page 170.
See *Gemstones of the World,* pages 110-113.

• TURQUOISE — $CuAl_6(PO_4)_4(OH)_8 \cdot 4H_2O$. Pale blue, blue-grey. Hardness 5-6.

Occurs in arid areas as a secondary mineral from the alteration of aluminum bearing surface rocks along with copper derived from the oxidation of copper sulfides, and phosphates probably derived from apatite. Related to hydrothermal copper deposits.

See Simon and Schuster's *Rocks and Minerals,* mineral no. 153.
See Golden *Rocks and Minerals,* page 244.
See *Gemstones of the World,* page 170.

• ZIRCON — $ZrSiO_4$. Many colors. Hardness 7.5.

Varieties include:

Jargoon — colorless, pale gray

Hyacinth — yellow, orange, red

These occur as an accessory mineral in silicic igneous rocks and their metamorphic derivatives. Also found in placers and beach sands derived from the above deposits.

See Simon and Schuster's *Rocks and Minerals,* mineral no. 165.
See Golden *Rocks and Minerals,* page 158.
See *Gemstones of the World,* page 108.

ADDITIONAL SEMIPRECIOUS GEMSTONES

• ANDALUSITE — $AlSiO_5$. Yellow, green, brown-red. Hardness 7.5.

Chiastolite — shows a dark internal cross. Hardness 5-5.5.

Occurs in low temperature, low pressure regional metamorphic rocks rich in Al and poor in Ca, K and Na.

See Simon and Schuster's *Rocks and Minerals,* mineral no. 167.
See Golden *Rocks and Minerals,* page 166.
See *Gemstones of the World,* page 178.

• APATITE — $Ca_5(PO_4)_3(OH,F,Cl)$. White, yellow, green, brown, blue. Hardness 5.

Occurs in pegmatites, hornfels and, as an accessory, in many igneous rocks.

See Simon and Schuster's *Rocks and Minerals,* mineral no. 140.
See Golden *Rocks and Minerals,* page 246
See *Gemstones of the World,* page 194.

• CALCITE — $CaCO_3$. Colorless, white, gray, yellow, red, green, blue, brown, black. Hardness 3.

Onyx Marble — banded calcite or aragonite

Occurs in hot springs or as stalactites or stalagmites in caverns. Also found in shear zones.

See Simon and Schuster's *Rocks and Minerals,* mineral nos. 93, 95.
See Golden *Rocks and Minerals,* pages 228, 232.
See *Gemstones of the World,* page 208.

• CORDIERITE — $Mg_2Al_4Si_5O_{18}$. Gray, blue or smoky. Hardness 7-7.5.

Occurs in hornfels and metaquartzite in contact metamorphic environments and hornfels and gneiss in regional metamorphic environments.

See Simon and Schuster's *Rocks and Minerals,* mineral no. 189.
See Golden *Rocks and Minerals,* page 172.
See *Gemstones of the World,* page 180.

• DIOPSIDE — $CaMgSi_2O_6$. Pale green, blue, white, yellow, brown. Hardness 5-6.

Varieties include:

Violane — purple
Lavrovite — dark green

These occur in marbles, hornfels and skarns in contact metamorphic environments and hornfels in regional metamorphic environments.

See Simon and Schuster's *Rocks and Minerals,* mineral no. 193.
See Golden *Rocks and Minerals,* page 176.
See *Gemstones of the World,* page 190.

• DIOPTASE — $CuSiO_2(OH)_2$. Emerald green. Hardness 5.

Occurs as a secondary copper mineral in the zone of oxidation of copper sulphide mineralization.

See Simon and Schuster's *Rocks and Minerals,* mineral no. 191.
See *Gemstones of the World,* page 194.

• EPIDOTE — $Ca_2(Al,Fe)_3Si_3O_{12}(OH)$. Pistachio green, black, red, yellow. Hardness 6-7.

Occurs in contact metamorphic rocks and medium grade regional metamorphic rocks of mafic composition. Also occurs in pegmatites and cavities in basalt with calcite and zeolites.

See Simon and Schuster's *Rocks and Minerals,* mineral no. 181.
See Golden *Rocks and Minerals,* page 160.
See *Gemstones of the World,* page 184.

• EUCLASE — $BeAlSiO_4(OH)$. Colorless, blue, green. Hardness 7.5.

Occurs in complex pegmatites and related placer deposits.

See Simon and Schuster's *Rocks and Minerals,* page 219.
See *Gemstones of the World,* page 178.

• HEMATITE — Fe_2O_3. Red to black. Hardness 5.5-6.5.

Specularite variety — black

Occurs in contact and regional metamorphic environments and in mesothermal and epithermal hydrothermal veins and replacement deposits.

See Simon and Schuster's *Rocks and Minerals,* mineral no. 65.
See Golden *Rocks and Minerals,* page 136.
See *Gemstones of the World,* page 162.

• KYANITE — Al_2SiO_5. Blue, white, gray, green, brown, black. Hardness 4-5, lengthwise; 6-7, crosswise.

Occurs in high grade regional metamorphic environments and less commonly in pegmatites.

See Simon and Schuster's *Rocks and Minerals,* mineral no. 168.
See Golden *Rocks and Minerals,* page 166.
See *Gemstones of the World,* page 196.

• MALACHITE — $Cu_2(CO_3)(OH)_2$. Green. Hardness 3.5-4.

Occurs as a secondary copper mineral in the oxide zone of copper deposits where sulphides react with carbonates.

See Simon and Schuster's *Rocks and Minerals,* mineral no. 100.
See Golden *Rocks and Minerals,* page 234.
See *Gemstones of the World,* page 176.

• RHODOCHROSITE — $MnCO_3$. Pink. Hardness 3.5-4.5.

Occurs in mesothermal veins and as a secondary mineral in the zone of oxidation of sulphide deposits.

See Simon and Schuster's *Rocks and Minerals,* mineral no. 92.
See Golden *Rocks and Minerals,* page 230.
See *Gemstones of the World,* page 168.

• RHODONITE — $(Mn,Fe,Mg)SiO_3$. Pink. Hardness 5.5-6.5.

Occurs in skarns in contact metamorphic environments and hydrothermal replacement deposits.

See Simon and Schuster's *Rocks and Minerals,* mineral no. 215.
See Golden *Rocks and Minerals,* page 178.
See *Gemstones of the World,* page 168.

• SILLIMANITE — Al_2SiO_5. Gray, brown, green, blue. Hardness 6-7.

Chatoyant — green and blue variety

Occurs in medium to high grade regional metamorphic environments, in contact metamorphic environments, and occasionally in pegmatites.

See Simon and Schuster's *Rocks and Minerals,* mineral no. 166.
See Golden *Rocks and Minerals,* page 166.
See *Gemstones of the World,* page 204.

• SPHENE (Titanite) — $CaTiSiO_5$. White, yellow-green, brown, black. Hardness 5-5.5.

Occurs in pegmatites as an accessory mineral in many silicic and intermediate intrusive and extrusive igneous rocks, in high grade regional metamorphic environments, and in contact metamorphic environments. It is also found in placers related to the above deposits.

See Simon and Schuster's *Rocks and Minerals,* mineral no. 172.
See *Gemstones of the World,* page 194.

• SPODUMENE — $LiAlSi_2O_6$. White, yellow, gray, pink, green. Hardness. 6.5-7.

Varieties include:
Hiddenite — emerald green
Kunzite — pink
These occur in lithium-bearing complex pegmatites.

See Simon and Schuster's *Rocks and Minerals,* mineral no. 200.
See Golden *Rocks and Minerals,* page 180.
See *Gemstones of the World,* page 114.

• VESUVIANITE (Idocrase) — $Ca_{10}Mg_2Al_4(SiO_4)_5(Si_2O_7)_2(OH)_4$. Brown, olive green, yellow, red, blue. Hardness 6.5.

Occurs in skarns in contact metamorphic environments and in serpentinized ultramafic rocks.

See Simon and Schuster's *Rocks and Minerals,* mineral no. 185.
See *Gemstones of the World,* page 186.

• ZOISITE — $Ca_2Al_3(Si_3O_{12})(OH)$. White, blue, pale green. Hardness 6-6.5.

Varieties include:

Thulite — pink
Tanzanite — violet pink

These occur in high grade regional metamorphic environments and in hornfels in contact metamorphic environments. Also found in hydrothermal veins associated with sulphides.

See Simon and Schuster's *Rocks and Minerals,* mineral no. 184.
See Golden *Rocks and Minerals,* page 160.
See *Gemstones of the World,* page 160.

TABLE 10-1
Gemstone Environment

Pegmatite	Mafic & Silica Deficient Igneous Rocks	Contact Metamorphic	Regional Metamorphic
Apatite	Diamond	Apatite	Almandine
Beryl	Labradorite	Cordierite	Andalusite
Chrysoberyl	Olivine (peridot)	Diopside	Diopside
Emerald	Pyrope	Epidote	Jadeite
Euclase	Ruby	Grossular	Kyanite
Moonstone	Sapphire	Lazurite	Nephrite
Quartz	Sodalite	Rhodonite	Sillimanite
Ruby	Uvarovite	Ruby	Staurolite
Sapphire	Zircon	Sapphire	Zoisite
Sphene		Sphene	
Spessartite		Spinel	
Spodumene		Tourmaline	
Topaz		Vesuvianite	
Tourmaline		Zoisite	

Hydrothermal Solutions	Descending Waters	Circulating Ground Water	Placer
Gold-quartz	Azurite	Agate	Almandine
Hematite	Calcite	Amethyst	Beryl
Quartz	Chrysocolla	Chalcedony	Chrysoberyl
Rhodochrosite	Dioptase	Jasper	Corundum
Rhodonite	Hematite	Opal	Diamond
Malachite	Quartz	Garnet	
Smithsonite	Spinel		
Turquoise	Sphene		
Topaz			
Tourmaline			
Zircon			

PART IV — Maps, Prospecting & Mining Claims

CHAPTER 11: Maps and Information

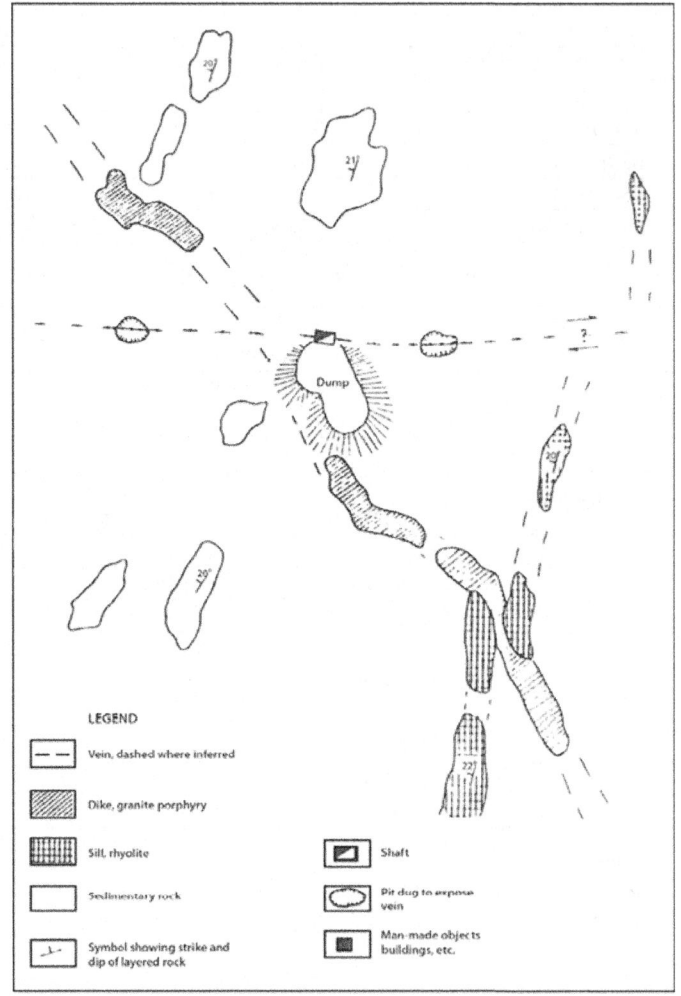

Example of a geologic outcrop map.
(From Earll, F.N., et al., *Handbook for Small Mining Enterprises*, Montana Bureau of Mines and Geology, Bulletin No. 99, March 1976.)

INTRODUCTION

A knowledge of maps and how to use them is necessary when you head for the hills to collect rocks and minerals or to go prospecting. Maps are nothing more than two-dimensional representations of specific geographic areas.

There are many different types of maps: some show topography, some show drainage, some show roads or land status, and some maps show geology.

TOPOGRAPHIC MAPS

The maps we are interested in should show the topography and drainage, the roads and trails and locations of mining activity. If we can get geologic maps of the area we are interested in, all the better. Learning to read and use maps is not difficult. It involves a knowledge of map symbols and use of the compass for determining direction. Some of the best maps available are published by the U.S. Geological Survey. A series of 2° maps at a scale of 1"=4 miles covers the entire United States as does a new 1:100,000 series. These are both excellent series for use as a general reference. The U.S. Geological Survey Quadrangle Series is excellent for detailed work. Map coverage is extensive for most western states, though not complete. Map scales are either 1"=1 mile or 2-l/2"=1 mile. At 1"=1 mile, the map is known as a 15° quadrangle sheet. At 2-l/2"=1 mile, it is a 7-1/2° quadrangle sheet. These maps are made from aerial photographs and then field checked. Accuracy is excellent and, with a little practice, you should be able to locate exactly where you are. See Figures 11-1, 11-2, 11-3 and 11-4.

FIGURE 11-1
Example of an AMS 2° USGS Topographic Map
(1 inch = 4 miles)

Scale 1:250,000
Contour Interval 200 feet

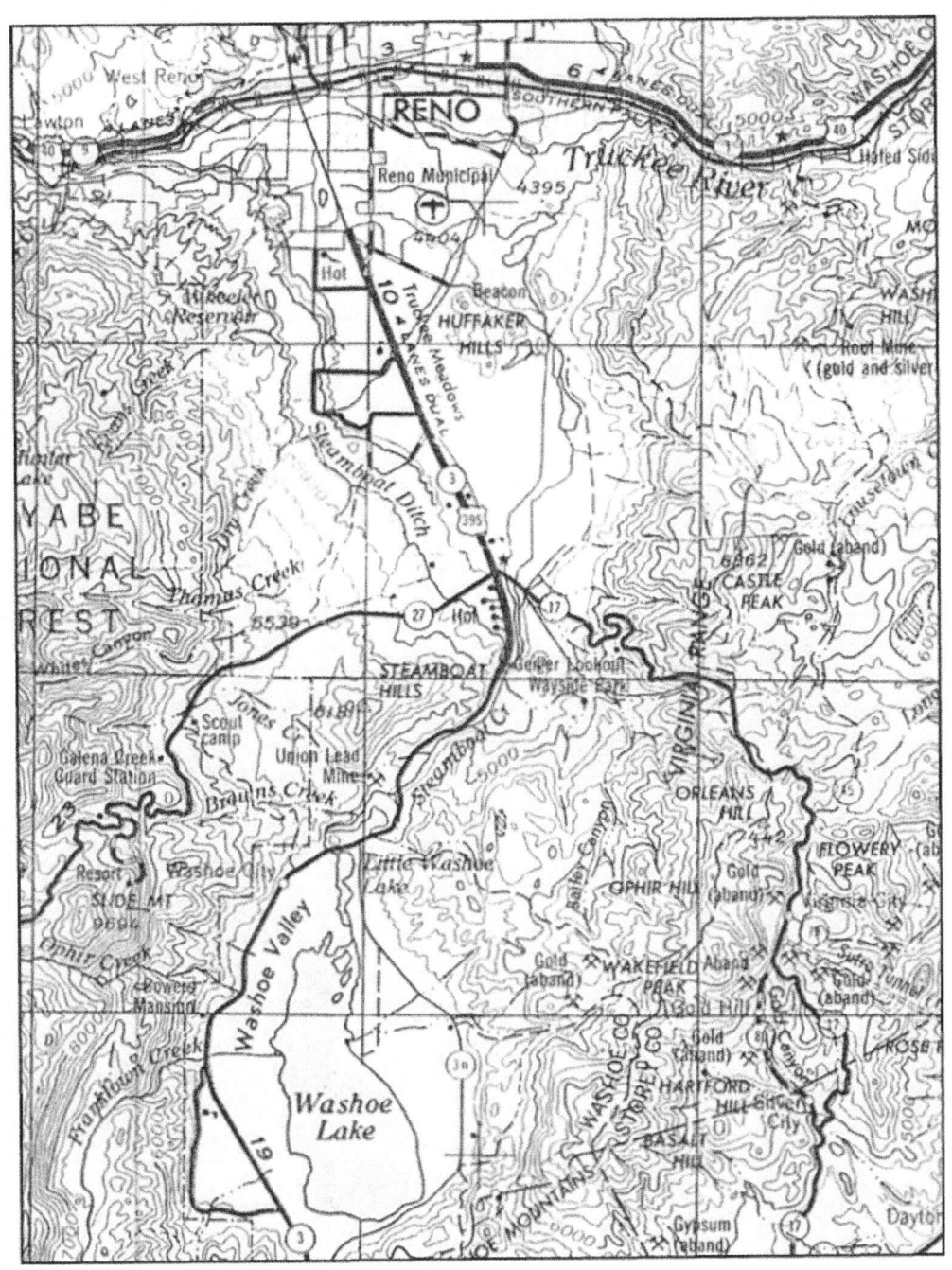

FIGURE 11-2
Example of USGs 1:100,000-Scale Metric Topographic Map
(1 inch = 1.6 miles)

Scale 1:100,000
Contour Interval 50 feet

FIGURE 11-3
Example of USGS 15 Minute Quadrangle Topographic Map
(1 Inch = 1 Mile)

Scale 1:62,500
Contour Interval 40 feet

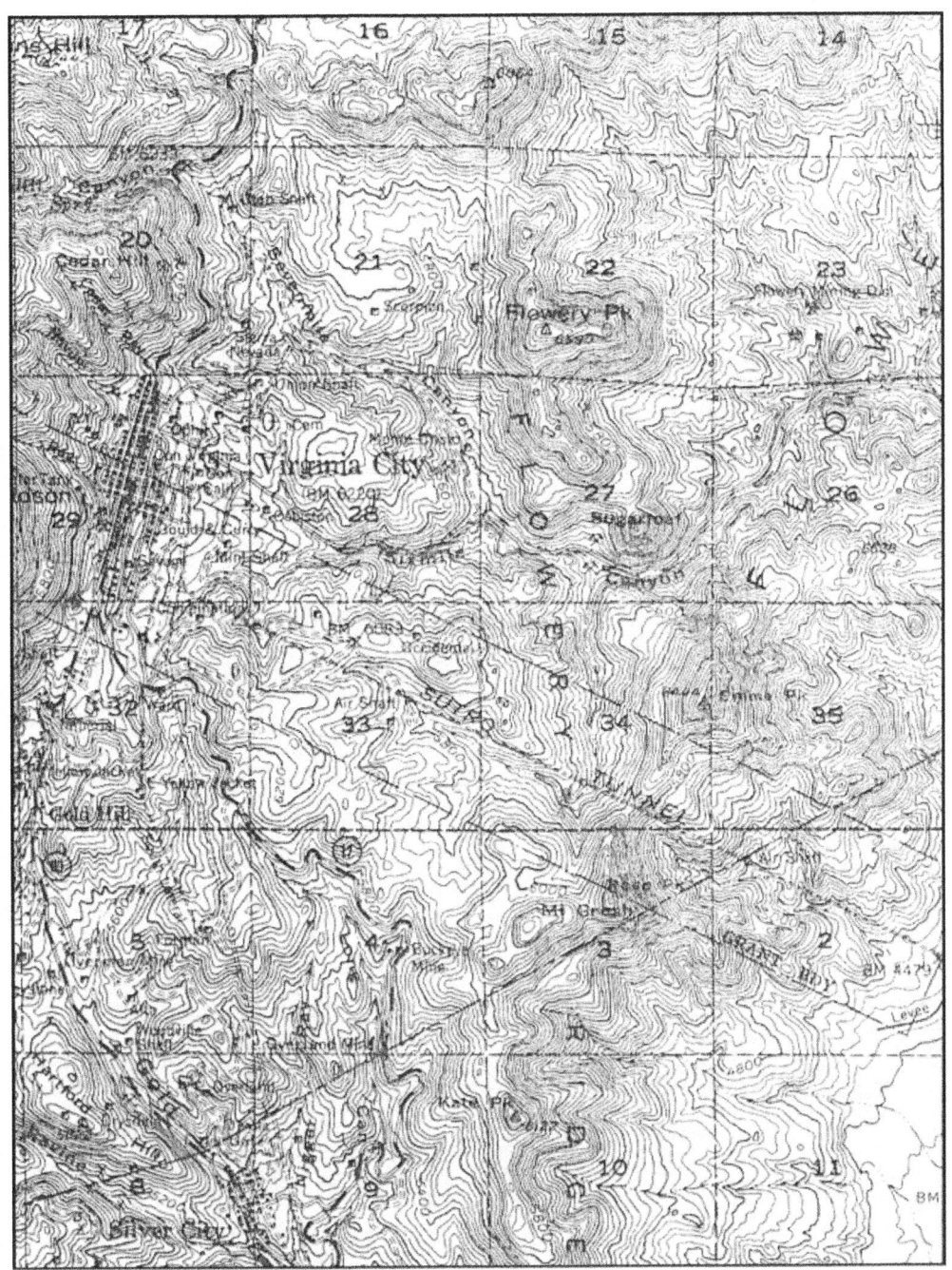

FIGURE 11-4
Example of USGS 7-1/2 Minute Quadrangle Topographic Map
(1 Inch = 2000 Feet) Feet)

Scale 1:24,000
Contour Interval 40 feet

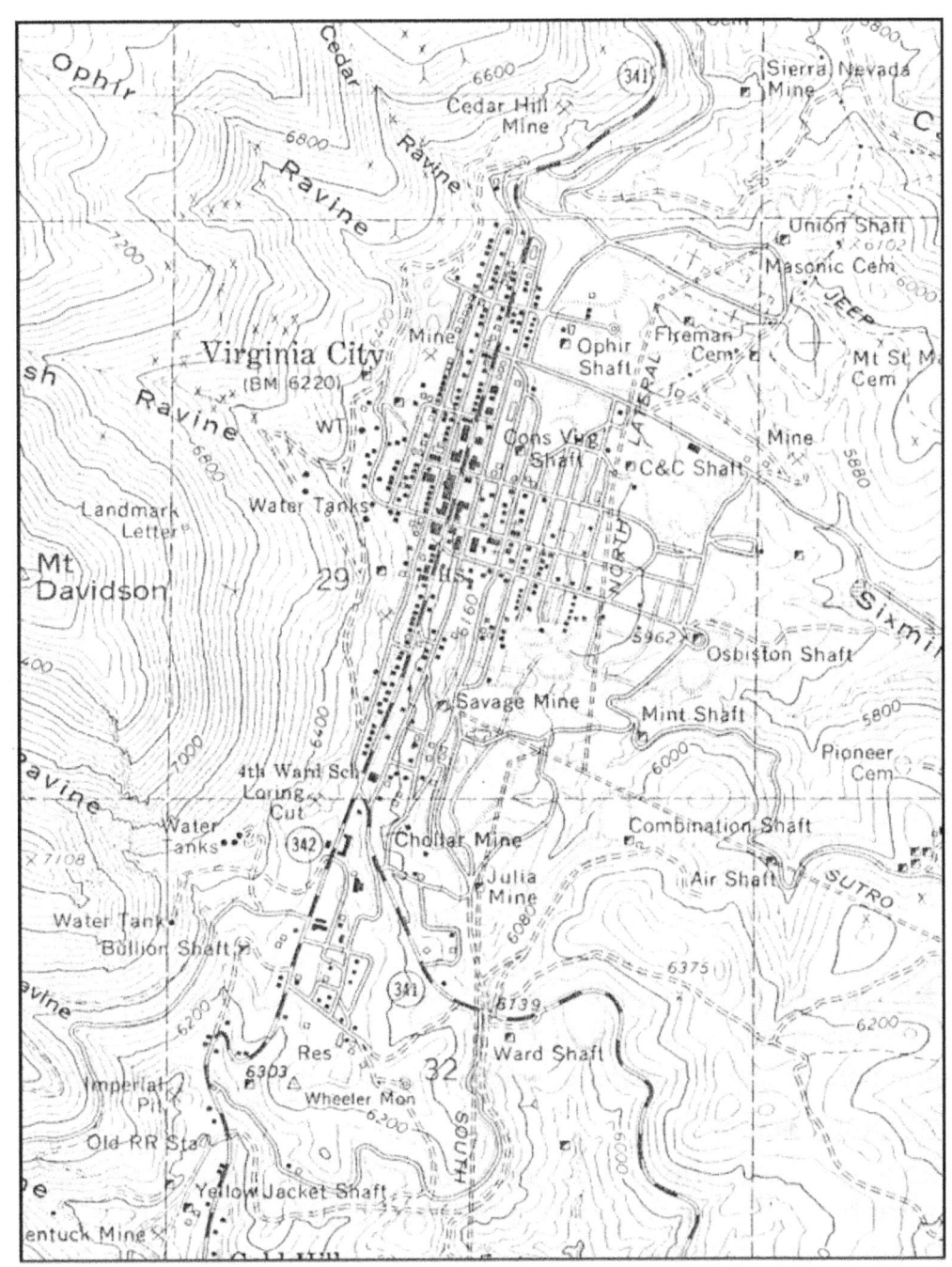

You can find your location by using bends in roads, intersections of roads, man-made objects, bends in streams, and particular landforms such as ridges, changes in slopes, or saddles.

These maps are inexpensive and readily available.

For the Western United States, the U.S. Geological Survey maps are available from the Federal Center in Denver, Colorado or from the USGS in Fairbanks, Alaska. For statewide areas in the Western United States, maps can be obtained at the Federal Public Inquiries offices.

Usually one or two businesses carry these USGS maps for local areas. The cost is a little more than the government price, but the convenience of a local source is worth it.

Other sources are the local city library, a university library or state Division of Mines offices. Topographic maps are also available on the internet at USGS.gov/locator. If you can find the map and area you want, just make a photocopy at the library.

Much of the Western United States has aerial photograph coverage. Where there is good quality photography, it is possible to locate the tree you are standing under. For aerial photo information and index coverage, contact the U.S. Geological Survey at Menlo Park, California. U.S. Soil Conservation offices also have aerial photo information.

For quick information about local map and photo coverage, you might contact your local U.S. Forest Service or BLM offices. There is usually a field employee or engineer available who can give you information in a few minutes time.

See *Prospecting for Gemstones and Minerals,* pages 6-22 and 362-367.

GEOLOGIC MAPS

Geologic maps show the geology usually overprinted on a topographic map. Rock types and structural features such as folds and faults are represented by colors, designs and symbols. An explanation can be found on the map listing the rock types and general structural features (see Figure 11-5).

FIGURE 11-5
Example of a Geologic Map
(From Nevada Bureau of Mines Bulletin 59, 1964)

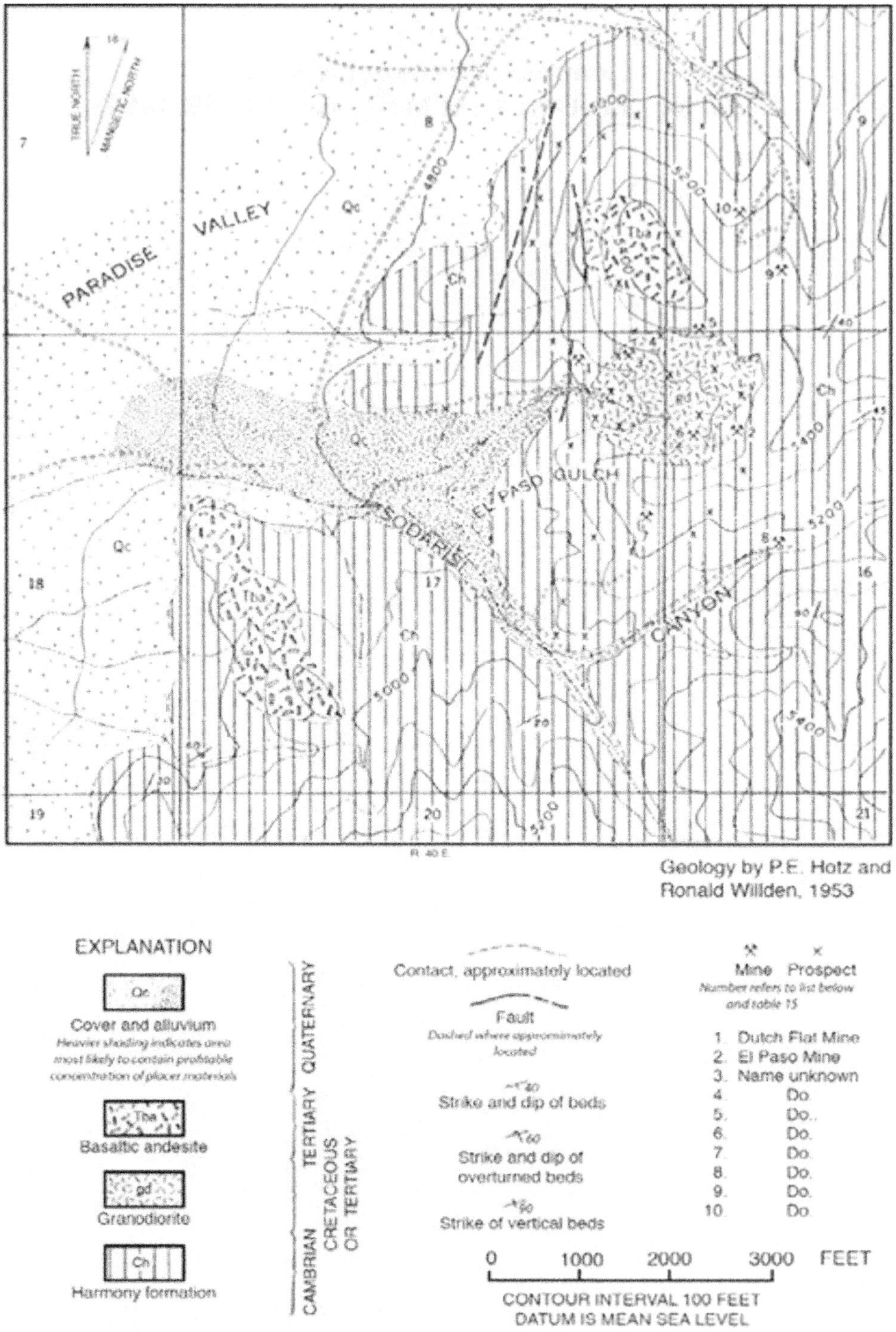

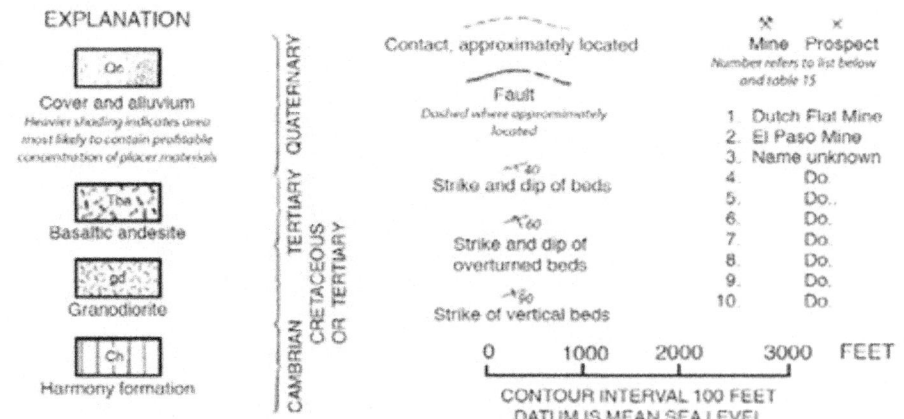

Geology by P.E. Hotz and
Ronald Willden, 1953

EXPLANATION

Qc

Cover and alluvium
*Heavier shading indicates area
most likely to contain profitable
concentration of placer materials*

Tba

Basaltic andesite

gd

Granodiorite

Ch

Harmony formation

QUATERNARY
TERTIARY

CRETACEOUS
OR TERTIARY

CAMBRIAN

Contact, approximately located

Fault
*Dashed where approximately
located*

40
Strike and dip of beds

60
Strike and dip of
overturned beds

90
Strike of vertical beds

Mine   Prospect
*Number refers to list below
and table 15*

1. Dutch Flat Mine
2. El Paso Mine
3. Name unknown
4. Do.
5. Do..
6. Do.
7. Do.
8. Do.
9. Do.
10. Do.

0   1000   2000   3000   FEET

CONTOUR INTERVAL 100 FEET
DATUM IS MEAN SEA LEVEL

140

A knowledge of the geologic time scale (see Table 11-1) is necessary to find and interpret the geologic environment you are looking for. An example would be if you are looking for a contact metamorphic environment, you would be looking for limestone or dolomite formations that were intruded by younger granitic rocks. If the limestone and dolomite formations were younger than the granitic rocks, it would indicate that they were either in fault contact, or the limestone and dolomite were deposited on the granite after it had cooled, been uplifted, eroded and subsided below sea level.

Often, geologic maps are part of a geologic report of a particular area which can give you additional information.

See *Prospecting for Gemstones and Minerals,* pages 11-12.

TABLE 11-1
Geologic Time Scale

Major Stratigraphic and Time Divisions
In Use by the U.S. Geological Survey

ERA	PERIOD	EPOCH	ESTIMATED AGES OF TIME BOUNDARIES (in millions of years)	DOMINANT LIFE FORMS
CENOZOIC	Quaternary	Recent		Animals and plant of modern types
			0.01	
		Pleistocene		
			3	
	Tertiary	Pliocene		
			7.5	Age of mammals and flowering plants
		Miocene		
			26	
		Oligocene		
			37	
		Eocene		
			54	
		Paleocene		
			65	——— Mass Extinction ———
MESOZOIC	Cretaceous	Upper (Late) Lower (Early)		
			140	
	Jurassic	Upper (Late) Middle (Middle) Lower (Early)		Age of reptiles, first birds, mammals and modern fishes
			205	
	Triassic	Upper (Late) Middle (Middle) Lower (Early)	220	——— Mass Extinction ———
			245	——— Mass Extinction ———
PALEOZOIC	Permian	Upper (Late) Lower (Early)		Age of amphibians, first reptiles
			250	
	Pennsylvanian	Upper (Late) Middle (Middle) Lower (Early)		
			325	Conifers, modern insects
	Mississippian	Upper (Late) Lower (Early		
			355	——— Mass Extinction ———
	Devonian	Upper (Late) Middle (Middle) Lower (Early)		Age of fishes
			415	——— Mass Extinction ———
	Silurian	Upper (Late) Middle (Middle) Lower (Early)		Shells dominant, first fishes
			440	
	Ordovician	Upper (Late) Middle (Middle) Lower (Early)		First vertebrates, first insects
			495	
	Cambrian	Upper (Late) Middle (Middle) Lower (Early)		Invertebrates dominant
			545	
PRECAMBRIAN				First invertebrates and plants

SOURCES OF GEOLOGIC INFORMATION

It never hurts to know as much as you can about an area you want to visit and it is surprising how much information is available if you just know where to look. Two main sources of information are the U.S. Geological Survey and the State Bureau of Mines and Geology.

The U.S. Geological Survey has an Index of Publications in two volumes to 1970 and then a yearly index. This can be picked up at any government public inquiries office or by mail from the Federal Center in Denver, Colorado.

These USGS publication indexes have a listing by state and county to help guide you to a specific area or mining district. Some of the older publications are no longer in print for purchase, but are probably available for review at a local university or college library or geological survey office.

Every state has a Department or Bureau of Mines and Geology with publications spanning many years. All offer free lists of publication and map prices. Again, older publications may be out of print, but available for review at the Bureau of Mines office, or even a local library. Usually these reports and maps can be photocopied. Every western state Bureau of Mines and Geology has a publication titled: "Mineral and Water Resources of (State)." This publication is an excellent compilation of information and references.

University Masters theses or Ph.D. dissertations are available for inspection at local colleges and universities. Usually a letter to the geology department is good for a free list of theses or dissertations and a review of the titles can give a hint of the area covered.

Magazines and journals often have articles of local interest and books may be published that give information on local or statewide areas.

See *Prospecting for Gemstones and Minerals,* pages 2-6 and 362-387.

CHAPTER 12:
Prospecting Techniques

INTRODUCTION

Prospecting for minerals, gemstones, rocks and rare or precious metal deposits can be for fun or profit. To get the most out of your time and effort, a logical plan should be followed.

First choose your objective: the particular minerals or rocks, or a reconnaissance of a particular area for whatever you can find. Next, obtain all available topographic maps and review all geologic reports and maps of the area. What rock types occur? What is the geologic environment? What minerals are likely to occur in the particular geologic environment? Be able to identify the minerals and rocks you expect to find. Note any past and present mining activity in the area and known collecting sites. Also, determine land status, if possible. Are you dealing with federal, state or private land?

To be remembered is that many old-timers roamed the hills and they had time, and they were patient, and probably covered nearly every square foot, discovering most everything obvious. However, they were not experts at identifying all minerals and gemstones and many had little or no geologic background, so some minerals and gemstones have gone unnoticed.

Wood print by Eduard Heuchler

PROSPECTING TECHNIQUES

There are a number of different prospecting techniques and much has been published on the subject. Included here are a few of the common ones.

Visual Reconnaissance — Getting over the area selected on foot, horseback or trailbike is the only way you can get close to what you are looking for. Pay attention to rock outcrops, rock float on soil-covered hillsides and gravels in stream channels. Particular attention should be directed to mine dumps and workings. Check the accuracy of geologic maps and search out the geologic environment you are seeking. Remember, it is human nature to see only what you want to see, so you must know what you are looking for.

See *Prospecting for Gemstones and Minerals,* pages 250 (bottom)-270 (top).

Panning Stream Gravels — Presence of heavy minerals and gemstones can be checked by panning stream gravels from place to place. If something of interest is found, it can be followed upstream to where you can no longer find it. You must then backtrack toward your last sampling site where the mineral or gemstone was present. Where you next pick up the mineral or gemstone, direct your search upslope from that point, panning the deeper soil and trace the mineral or gemstone up until you find the outcrop, or if buried, the place to dig.

This basic prospecting method has been used by the old-time prospectors for over a hundred years.

Ultra-violet Prospecting — Certain minerals can be easily identified when observed under the ultra-violet lamp. Calcite and scheelite are two examples. Prospecting must be done at night and care must be taken in getting around. An interesting side feature is that scorpions and rattlesnakes show up beautifully under ultra-violet light.

See *Prospecting for Gemstones and Minerals,* page 270-273 (bottom).

Radioactivity Prospecting — Minerals containing uranium and thorium will respond to a scintillation counter or Geiger counter. Scintillation counters detect high energy particles and Geiger counters detect gamma radiation given off by radioactive material.

See *Prospecting for Gemstones and Minerals,* page 273 (bottom)-275 (top).

Geochemical Sampling — More sophisticated prospecting includes geochemical sampling. Generally used in base and precious metal exploration, samples of stream sediment, soil, or rocks are obtained and analyzed for trace elements. The results are plotted and can be used as a guide to an area for detailed work.

Assaying — Samples collected are sent to an assay laboratory and analyzed for whatever you want. Most labs provide, without charge, a list of services and costs.

Geophysical Prospecting — Expensive and usually restricted to use by mining companies or the government. There are a number of different geophysical methods of prospecting. These methods measure magnetic, resistance, or electrical properties of rocks and minerals. There is a relationship between magnetic and electrical properties in rocks and sulphide mineralization that can be used to locate drilling targets.

CHAPTER 13:
Protecting Your Find

INTRODUCTION

Assume your prospecting pays off; you find something of value. How do you protect your find? Answering this question depends on what you found and where you found it.

First, locate your find on a map, preferably a USGS topographic map. This will give you information as to section, township and county you are in. Also check the field area of your find for signs of recent work, and mining claim posts. If you find claim posts, look for location notices, which will give you the name and address of the locator, name of the claim, and the date of location. With this information you can determine the land status and who you have to deal with.

LAND STATUS

There are three major classifications of land: privately owned land, state owned land, and land belonging to the federal government. Land status maps for most states are available through either the State Bureau of Mines or the Federal Bureau of Land Management offices. These maps designate land status as private, state or federal, using section and township for location.

For private ownership, check the county tax records in the county where the land is located. Once the name and address of the owner is known, you can hunt up the recorded deed for the exact boundary description. You should be able to trace back the chain of title to the original grant or homestead to determine where the mineral rights lie. The mineral rights have either been reserved in the federal government or state, have been retained by a past owner, or have passed with the land to the present owner.

If mineral rights lie with a past or present owner of the land, you must deal exclusively with that party on either a lease or purchase basis, if they want to deal at all.

If mineral rights lie with the state, you must deal with the state Land Board or Department, usually on a lease basis. This will involve a written lease agreement with the state, subject to state rules and regulations.

If your find is on federal land, what you do depends on what you find and what the particular federal land classification is where your find is located. Table 13-1 lists the various metals, minerals and rocks, and federal land classification. With leasable and salable material, you must deal directly with the federal government, either the local Bureau of Land Management or Forest Service offices. Procedures in booklet form are available from these agencies. If your find is locatable as a mining claim on federal land, or private, or state land in which the government has retained mineral rights, your first task should be to check that there are no existing unpatented or patented claims covering your find. Check the area for 4"x4" posts, PVC plastic pipes, rock piles or tree stumps used for marking claim boundaries, and recent dozer or excavation work. If you suspect there might be existing claims, look for the location notice, which may be in an old tobacco can, a glass jar, a beer can, or even inserted in a drilled-out hole in a 4"x4" post.

If you find the location notice, you can check the BLM master title plats by Section and Township to determine whether or not a patented mining claim covers your find. Also check the BLM and county recorder's records to determine if there is an active unpatented mining claim covering your find. You can do this by the name of the claim and location, and whether or not the required notice of yearly assessment work has been filed.

Since 1979, location certificates of all unpatented mining claims must be filed, along with a map of the claims, with the Bureau of Land Management in the state office of the state in which the claim is located. The BLM has prepared master indexes listing all claims by geography, name of claim, or name of owner on microfiche which can be purchased.

If you know the section, township and range, you can go to the microfiche for the list of claims in the section. Each claim shows a lead file number which can be used to obtain the file in the BLM State Office which has a map of the claim. The map should show the near/exact location of the claim in the section.

A copy of the Notice of Assessment must be filed with the BLM state office on or before December 30 of each year. A check of the microfiche will tell you if the claim is current.

LOCATING A MINING CLAIM

If your preliminary work shows no existing claims covering your find, and the area is open to mineral entry, you may locate your own mining claim if you have made a discovery of a valuable mineral deposit. The mineral, metal and rocks that can be claimed are listed in Table 13-1.

A discovery has been defined as a mineral deposit of such value that it can be mined, removed and disposed of at a profit by a person of ordinary prudence.

TABLE 13-1
Locatable, Leasable and Salable Mineral Status

	Locatable Minerals[1]	Leaseable Minerals[2]	Salable Minerals[3]
FEDERAL LANDS			
BLM	Yes	Yes	Yes
National Forest	Yes	Yes	Yes
National Recreation Area	No	No	No
Primitive-Wilderness	Yes[4]	Yes[4]	Yes[4]
Indian Reservation	No	No	No
STATE LAND	Yes	Yes	No
PRIVATE LAND	No[5]	No[5]	No[5]

[1] LOCATABLE MINERALS & METALS: All valuable mineral deposits, excluding leasable and salable minerals.

[2] LEASABLE MINERALS: Coal, potassium and sodium, phosphate, tar sand, oil and gas, geothermal steam, and others.

[3] SALABLE MINERALS: Common varieties of sand, gravel, stone, pumicite and cinders and others.

[4] To a certain future date Dec. 31, 1983, for some, and later dates for others.

[5] Unless reserved in U.S.

There are two types of mining claims: lode claims and placer claims. Lode claims are used to cover lodes or veins of mineral in solid rock. Typical placer deposits in sands and gravels are located using placer claims. If any question exists, use both lode and placer claims to cover the same ground to protect yourself.

Mining law is a combination of federal law and state law. Federal law requires that there be a discovery within the limits of the lode claim, which may not exceed 1,500 feet by 600 feet (20 acres) and that the claim be marked on the ground so that its boundaries can be traced. A placer claim can be no larger than 20 acres, usually 1,320 feet by 660 feet. Association of locators, from two to eight persons, may locate a single placer claim of 20 acres for each individual in the association, up to 160 acres.

State law generally covers how the claim boundaries are to be marked, performance of the required discovery work, and recording of the location notices, or a location certificate within a certain period.

The Bureau of Mines and Geology in most states has published booklets of that state's mining laws. It is extremely important that the mining laws of the state in which your find is located are reviewed for the exact procedures to be used.

In addition to the above laws governing mining claims, the BLM and Forest Service have regulations which are related to the work done on your claim. You may have to present a mining plan for approval that describes surface work you intend to do.

In locating a claim, fill out a Location Notice and post it up on PVC plastic pipe,[*] a 4x4 post or rock pile at your discovery. You then have 60 to 90 days to record the Location Notice or Certificate of Location in the county courthouse in the county where your claim is located. You must also put up claim corner posts or rock piles within 60 to 90 days to mark the boundary of your claim. States vary as to the number of posts. Some require four, some six, with two side center posts, or two end center posts. A copy of the Location Notice must be filed with the BLM State Office within 90 days of location of the claim.

 * PVC plastic pipe is being outlawed in many states because of environmental problems related to birds and small animals becoming trapped inside the plastic pipe.

Discovery work within 60 to 90 days is required in a few states, and varies from excavations to particular maps of your claim that are filed with the state.

To keep your claim valid, you must perform at least $100 assessment work on or related to each claim prior to September 1 each year, and file a Notice of Assessment Work within 60 days in the county courthouse, as well as on or before December 30 with the BLM state office.

In 1993, the federal government changed the laws regarding assessment work. With some exceptions, the law now requires a prepaid rental of $100 per claim instead of $100 in assessment work.

If your discovery is questionable, the federal government may challenge the validity of your claim. If this happens, you will receive notice and be entitled to a hearing, which is one of your due-process rights.

If you have a valid discovery of economically marketable ore or mineral, you may want to apply for patent to obtain absolute title to your claim. Patenting a mining claim is a somewhat complex process, including surveying the claim and filing proper paperwork. It is best to see an attorney familiar with patenting mining claims for the information necessary to make the decision. It should be noted that very few claims go to patent today because of the hassle and cost involved.

It should be noted that there is a push on in Congress to revise the federal mining laws and that there will probably be some changes within the next few years (mid- to late-1900s).

GOOD HUNTING!

PART V — Appendices

GLOSSARY

Accessory Mineral — A mineral found in a rock in such minor quantities that its presence does not affect the way the rock is named or classified.

Acidic Igneous Rock — Igneous rock consisting predominantly of light colored minerals and more than 66 percent silica (combined and/or quartz). "Silicic" is presently used rather than the word "acidic."

Alluvial Deposit — Sedimentary deposit formed from deposition in water.

Alteration — Any physical or chemical change in a mineral or rock subsequent to original formation.

Amorphous — Noncrystalline.

Amygdaloidal — A volcanic rock (usually basalt) containing numerous gas cavities filled with secondary minerals such as calcite, quartz or zeolites.

Aphanitic Texture — An igneous rock in which the mineral constituents are too small to be seen with the naked eye.

Aplite — A variety of granite that is fine-grained with a sugary appearance; usually found in dikes and associated with pegmatites.

Basalt — Common black lava.

Base Metal — The common metals, such as copper, lead, zinc, etc., excluding iron.

Basement Rock — The older crystalline rock mass beneath a series of sedimentary rocks.

Basic Igneous Rock — Old term referring to a dark colored igneous rock with low silica content and a high percentage of minerals rich in iron and magnesium. The term "mafic" is now generally used in place of "basic."

Batholith — Body of plutonic rock that has been intruded deep into the earth's crust which has been later eroded, exposing an area of greater than 40 square miles.

Bedding — The arrangement of sedimentary rocks in approximately parallel layers.

Blueschist — A metamorphic rock that forms at high pressure and low temperature.

Breccia — Rock composed of angular fragments.

Calcareous — Containing calcium carbonate (calcite).

Caliche — A white calcareous crust found at or near the surface in arid regions, formed from the evaporation of rain water.

Carbonaceous — Composed largely of organic carbon.

Carbonatite — Rare intrusive composed of calcite and dolomite.

Cleavage — Mineral breakage along one or more regular, smooth surfaces.

Conglomerate — A sedimentary rock consisting of rounded or semi-rounded cemented cobbles, sand and gravel.

Contact Metamorphic Zone — Zone of rock surrounding a hot igneous intrusive that has undergone mineralogic change because of heat, minor pressure and the possible addition of chemical constituents.

Country Rock — Unmineralized rock surrounding ore deposits.

Crystal — Solid mineral body with regular atomic structure and flat external surfaces.

Detrital Sediment — A deposit of mineral and rock fragments that have been transported to their place of deposition.

Diagenesis — The final process of forming a sedimentary rock from a sediment.

Dike — Intrusive igneous rock injected across the layers of surrounding rocks.

Element — A substance which cannot be decomposed into other substances.

Epithermal Vein — A vein formed at shallow depths from ascending hydrothermal solutions.

Essential Mineral — The mineral constituents of a rock that are used to classify and name the rock.

Evaporite — Sedimentary rock or mineral of chemical origin formed by the evaporation of water.

Extrusive Rock — Igneous rock that solidifies on the surface of the earth.

Fault — A break in the earth's crust with relative movement of the rocks on both sides.

Feldspar — A group of abundant rock forming silicate minerals in most igneous and metamorphic rocks.

Feldspathoids — A group of minerals that are similar in composition to feldspars but contain less silica, occurring in silica deficient (no quartz) igneous rocks (leucite, nepheline, sodalite).

Fissile — Ability to break up into thin flat sheets, such as shale.

Fold — Deformation of rock strata into folds (anticlines or synclines) as a result of compressional forces.

Foliation — The laminated structure seen in regionally metamorphosed rocks, caused from segregation of different minerals into roughly parallel layers.

Fractionation — The segregation of minerals or chemical components during magmatic crystallization, producing different rock types from the same magma.

Fracture — Irregular breakage of mineral or rock.

Gangue — The waste rock or noneconomic components of a mineral deposit.

Gel — A semi-solid colloidal solution.

Geode — A hollow concretion lined with crystals often found in sedimentary and volcanic rocks.

Geology — The science which deals with the study of the earth.

Gneiss — A metamorphic rock of light and dark-colored bands (pronounced "nice").

Gossan — The iron oxide outcrop of a sulphide vein.

Granite — A common medium to coarse-grained intrusive igneous rock composed of feldspar, quartz and minor black minerals. The term granite is often casually used to refer to any light coarse-grained intrusive igneous rock when the rock name is not known.

Granitic Texture — A term generally referring to the coarse-grained texture of intrusive igneous rocks.

Greisen — Granite which has been altered by the action of fluids rich in volatile elements. Often related to tin deposits.

Groundmass (Matrix) — The fine-grained material that surrounds phenocrysts (larger crystals) in a porphyritic rock.

Hardness — The resistance of a mineral to scratching and abrasion measured by the Mohs Scale.

Hydrothermal Alteration — The alteration of minerals or rocks by the action of hydrothermal solutions.

Hydrothermal Replacement — Change in a rock or mineral deposit due to the addition or removal of minerals by hydrothermal solutions.

Hydrothermal Solutions — Hot metal and ion bearing solutions originating within a crystallizing magma.

Hypothermal Vein — A vein formed at fairly great depth and at relatively high temperatures from hydrothermal solutions.

Igneous Rock — A rock formed by the crystallization of magma or lava.

Intrusive Rock — An igneous rock that formed below the earth's surface from magma that was squeezed into and between layers of older rock.

Laterite — A highly leached soil, which can be enriched in iron or aluminum. Found in tropical climates.

Lava — Molten rock material extruded onto the earth's surface through a volcano.

Leaching Zone — Zone in the upper part of a mineral deposit where chemical components are leached.

Limestone — A type of sedimentary rock composed chiefly of the mineral calcite. Most limestones were deposited in shallow seas and contain fossils.

Lithification — The change of a sediment into solid rock.

Lode Deposit — A deposit of valuable minerals (usually metals in bedrock).

Luster — A reflective property of mineral surfaces.

Mafic Rocks — Igneous rock consisting of abundant ferromagnesium minerals (45-52% silica) giving the rock a dark color.

Magma — Molten rock material below the earth's surface.

Matrix — See groundmass.

Mesothermal Vein — A vein that forms at intermediate depth and temperature.

Metamorphic Facies — A set of temperature and pressure conditions under which a suite of metamorphic minerals and resulting rock is formed from pre-existing rock of any type.

Metamorphic Rock — Any rock formed from pre-existing rocks through heat, pressure and the effects of superheated solutions.

Metasomatism — Process of changing the composition of minerals and adding or removing minerals by the addition and removal of chemical elements or components in an exchange process involving fluids.

Miarolitic Cavity — Small angular cavities in granitic rocks and pegmatites, often lined with crystals.

Mineral — A homogeneous substance, composed of a specific chemical composition, and produced by natural inorganic processes.

Mineral Deposit — A concentration of one or more economically valuable minerals.

Mohs Hardness Scale — A relative scale of the hardness of minerals, arbitrarily reading from 1 to 10.

Molecule — Smallest amount of a compound having all its chemical properties.

Ore — Rock or mineral which can be mined at a profit.

Outcrop — Surface exposure of the underlying rock.

Oxidized Zone — The upper part of an ore body that has been altered by downward percolating ground water, containing dissolved oxygen and carbon dioxide.

Pegmatite — An intrusive igneous rock, granitic in composition, of extremely coarse-grain size. Usually found as dikes within a larger plutonic or metamorphic rock mass.

Petrology — The study of rocks, their composition, origin and modes of occurrence.

Phenocryst — Larger mineral surrounded by smaller mineral grains (groundmass or matrix) in a porphyritic rock.

Placer — A deposit of valuable minerals in stream gravels or beach sands.

Pluton — Any deep, intrusive igneous body.

Plutonic Rock — A granular igneous rock that has solidified at great depth.

Porphyritic Rock — An igneous rock in which larger crystals (phenocrysts) are enclosed in a fine-grained groundmass (matrix).

Precious Metal — Gold, silver or platinum.

Replacement Deposit — Mineral deposit where the original rock and mineral constituents have been replaced with new minerals and metals that give the deposit value.

Residual Mineral — A mineral that has resisted the alteration processes that disintegrate rocks.

Rock — A natural aggregate of one or more minerals.

Sandstone — A sedimentary rock composed of cemented sand-sized grains.

Secondary Enriched Zone — A portion of a mineralized zone beneath the leached zone and usually found at the water table at the time of leaching.

Secondary Minerals — Minerals formed by the alteration of pre-existing minerals.

Sediment — Unconsolidated rock and mineral material.

Sedimentary Rock — A layered rock formed through the accumulation and solidification of sediments, or through chemical precipitation.

Silicic Rock — See acidic igneous rock.

Specific Gravity — A measure of density; ratio of the mass of a mineral to the mass of an equal volume of water.

Stock — A body of plutonic rock that has been intruded deep into the earth's crust which has been later eroded, exposing an area of less than 40 square miles.

Stratification — Bedding in sedimentary rock.

Streak — Color of powdered mineral.

Structure — Large features of rock masses, such as bedding and flow banding, folding and faulting.

Texture — The appearance of a rock or mineral; the size, shape and interrelations of the crystals and other components.

Thin Section — A transparent slice of rock mounted on a glass slide.

Ultramafic Rock — Igneous rock very high in mafic minerals (less than 45% silica), giving the rock a very dark color.

Vein — A sheetlike body of mineral matter cutting across pre-existing rock.

Vesicle — A small cavity in a volcanic rock.

Vitreous — Glasslike in appearance or texture.

Volcano — A vent or hole in the earth's crust through which magma, gases and ash escape onto the surface.

Weathering — Processes that cause solid rock to decay into soil.

DETERMINATIVE TABLES

TABLE VIEWING OPTIONS

We present our Determinative Tables in two forms to let you choose your reading preference. The Table View represents the original layout from our print editions. This is followed by the Searchable Text View, which will allow you to use your search window to cross-reference to all other related segments of this book.

DETERMINATIVE TABLES
METALLIC or SUBMETALLIC LUSTER

HARDNESS Less Than 2.5
(will leave mark on paper)

table view

DETERMINATIVE TABLES
METALLIC or SUBMETALLIC LUSTER

Color	Streak	Hardness	Sp. Gr.	Remarks	Name & Formula	Geologic Environment
HARDNESS Less Than 2.5 (will leave mark on paper)						
Gray-Black	Black	1 to 1.5	2.3	Greasy feel	GRAPHITE C	Regional metamorphic
Blue-Gray	Blue-Gray	1 to 1.5	4.7	One good cleavage. Can be platy	MOLYBDENITE MoS_2	Granite and contact metamorphic
Black	Black	1 to 2	4.7	Fibrous aggregates	PYROLUSITE MnO_2	Oxide and secondary zone. Sea floor nodules
Blue	Gray	1.5 to 2	4.6	Platy masses or coatings. Can be iridescent	COVELLITE CuS	Secondary copper
Gray	Gray	2	4.6	One good cleavage. Crystals and cleavage elongated	STIBNITE Sb_2S_3	Low temperature hydrothermal
Gray	Gray	2 to 2.5	7.3	Sectile	ARGENTITE Ag_2S	Low temperature hydrothermal
Lead Gray	Gray	2.5	7.6	Cubic crystals and cleavage	GALENA PbS	Medium temperature hydrothermal
Black with Dark Red Tint	Purplish	2.5	5.8	Good cleavage. Ruby silver	PYRARGYRITE Ag_3SbS_3	Secondary silver

HARDNESS Less Than 2.5
(will leave mark on paper)

searchable text view

Hardness: 1 to 1.5; **Specific Gravity:** 2.3
Name / Formula: GRAPHITE / C
Geologic Environment: Regional metamorphic
Color: Gray-Black; **Streak:** Black
Remarks: Greasy feel

Hardness: 1 to 1.5; **Specific Gravity:** 4.7
Name / Formula: MOLYBDENITE / MoS_2

Geologic Environment: Granite and contact metamorphic
Color: Blue-Gray; **Streak:** Blue-Gray
Remarks: One good cleavage. Can be platy

Hardness: 1 to 2; **Specific Gravity:** 4.7
Name / Formula: PYROLUSITE / MnO_2

Geologic Environment: Oxide and secondary zone. Sea floor nodules
Color: Black; **Streak:** Black
Remarks: Fibrous aggregates

Hardness: 1.5 to 2; **Specific Gravity:** 4.6
Name / Formula: COVELLITE / CuS
Geologic Environment: Secondary copper
Color: Blue; **Streak:** Gray
Remarks: Platy masses or coatings. Can be iridescent

Hardness: 2; **Specific Gravity:** 4.6
Name / Formula: STIBNITE / Sb_2S_3
Geologic Environment: Low temperature hydrothermal
Color: Gray; **Streak:** Gray
Remarks: One good cleavage. Crystals and cleavage elongated

Hardness: 2 to 2.5; **Specific Gravity:** 7.3
Name / Formula: ARGENTITE / Ag_2S
Geologic Environment: Low temperature hydrothermal
Color: Gray; **Streak:** Gray
Remarks: Sectile

Hardness: 2.5; **Specific Gravity:** 7.6
Name / Formula: GALENA / PbS
Geologic Environment: Medium temperature hydrothermal
Color: Lead Gray; **Streak:** Gray
Remarks: Cubic crystals and cleavage

Hardness: 2.5; **Specific Gravity:** 5.8
Name / Formula: PYRARGYRITE / Ag_3SbS_3
Geologic Environment: Secondary silver
Color: Black with Dark Red Tint; **Streak:** Purplish
Remarks: Good cleavage. Ruby silver

DETERMINATIVE TABLES
METALLIC or SUBMETALLIC LUSTER

HARDNESS 2.5 to 5.5
(can be scratched with a knife)

table view

DETERMINATIVE TABLES
METALLIC or SUBMETALLIC LUSTER

Color	Streak	Hardness	Sp. Gr.	Remarks	Name & Formula	Geologic Environment
HARDNESS 2.5 to 5.5 (can be scratched with a knife)						
Gray-Black	Gray-Black	2.5 to 3	5.7	Can be sooty. Associated with malachite	CHALCOCITE Cu_2S	Secondary copper
Copper-Red	Copper-Red	2.5 to 3	8.9	Malleable. Tarnishes black	COPPER Cu	Secondary copper
Silver-White	Silver-White	2.33 to 3	10.5	Malleable. Tarnishes black	SILVER Ag	Low temperature hydrothermal or secondary silver
Gold-Yellow	Gold-Yellow	2.5 to 3	15.6-19.3	Malleable	GOLD Au	Hydrothermal with quartz; placer
Gray-Black	Black	3	4.4	Shows cleavage	ENARGITE Cu_3AsS_4	Medium temperature hydrothermal
Brownish-Bronze	Black	3	5.1	Tarnishes purple. Peacock ore	BORNITE Cu_5FeS_4	Medium temperature hydrothermal
Brass-Yellow	Black	3 to 3.5	5.4	Often in radiating hair-like crystals	MILLERITE NiS	Low temperature hydrothermal
Gray-Black	Black to Red	3 to 4.5	4.7-5.0	Usually massive	TETRAHEDRITE $(Cu,Fe)_{12}Sb_4S_{13}$	Low-medium temperature hydrothermal
Red, Brown, Black	Yellow-Brown	3.5 to 4	3.9-4.1	Ruby with no iron. Darker with more iron. Resinous luster	SPHALERITE ZnS	Medium temperature hydrothermal

HARDNESS 2.5 to 5.5
(can be scratched with a knife)

searchable text view

Hardness: 2.5 to 3; **Specific Gravity:** 5.7
Name / Formula: CHALCOCITE / Cu_2S
Geologic Environment: Secondary copper
Color: Gray-Black; **Streak:** Gray-Black
Remarks: Can be sooty.
Associated with malachite

Hardness: 2.5 to 3; **Specific Gravity:** 8.9
Name / Formula: COPPER / Cu
Geologic Environment: Secondary copper
Color: Copper-Red; **Streak:** Copper-Red
Remarks: Malleable. Tarnishes black

Hardness: 2.33 to 3; **Specific Gravity:** 10.5

Name / Formula: SILVER / Ag
Geologic Environment: Low temperature hydrothermal or secondary silver
Color: Silver-White; **Streak:** Silver-White
Remarks: Malleable. Tarnishes black

Hardness: 2.5 to 3; **Specific Gravity:** 15.6-19.3
Name / Formula: GOLD / Au
Geologic Environment: Hydrothermal with quartz; placer
Color: Gold-Yellow; **Streak:** Gold-Yellow
Remarks: Malleable

Hardness: 3; **Specific Gravity:** 4.4
Name / Formula: ENARGITE / Cu_3AsS_4
Geologic Environment: Medium temperature hydrothermal
Color: Gray-Black; **Streak:** Black
Remarks: Shows cleavage

Hardness: 3; **Specific Gravity:** 5.1
Name / Formula: BORNITE / Cu_5FeS_4
Geologic Environment: Medium temperature hydrothermal
Color: Brownish-Bronze; **Streak:** Black
Remarks: Tarnishes purple.
Peacock ore

Hardness: 3 to 3.5; **Specific Gravity:** 5.4
Name / Formula: MILLERITE / NiS
Geologic Environment: Low temperature hydrothermal
Color: Brass-Yellow; **Streak:** Black
Remarks: Often in radiating hair-like crystals

Hardness: 3 to 4.5; **Specific Gravity:** 4.7-5.0
Name / Formula: TETRAHEDRITE / $(Cu,Fe)_{12}Sb_4S_{13}$
Geologic Environment: Low-medium temperature hydrothermal
Color: Gray-Black; **Streak:** Black to Red
Remarks: Usually massive

Hardness: 3.5 to 4; **Specific Gravity:** 3.9-4.1
Name / Formula: SPHALERITE / ZnS
Geologic Environment: Medium temperature hydrothermal
Color: Red, Brown, Black; **Streak:** Yellow-Brown
Remarks: Ruby with no iron. Darker with more iron. Resinous luster

DETERMINATIVE TABLES
METALLIC or SUBMETALLIC LUSTER

HARDNESS 2.5 to 5.5
(can be scratched with a knife)

table view

DETERMINATIVE TABLES
METALLIC or SUBMETALLIC LUSTER

Color	Streak	Hardness	Sp. Gr.	Remarks	Name & Formula	Geologic Environment
Brass-Yellow	Black	3.5 to 4	4.3	Yellower than pyrite	CHALCOPYRITE $CuFeS_2$	Medium temperature hydrothermal
Black	Gray to Black	4	4.4	Sooty, fibrous	MANGANITE $MnO(OH)$	Low temperature hydrothermal
Bronze	Black	4	4.6	Slightly magnetic	PYRRHOTITE FeS	High temperature hydrothermal; mafic magmatic segregation
Silver-White	Gray	4 to 4.5	14-19	Malleable	PLATINUM Pt	Mafic magmatic segregation; placer
Black to Gray	Yellow-Brown	5 to 5.5	3.5	Botryoidal. Radiating crystals	GOETHITE $FeO(OH)$	Zone of oxidation
Black	Brown to Black	5 to 6	4.8	Platy crystals, massive. Slightly magnetic	ILMENITE $FeTiO_3$	Mafic, magmatic segregation; high temperature hydrothermal, pegmatite, placer
Black	Brown to Black	5 to 6	8-11	Pitchy luster, massive, radioactive	URANINITE UO_2	Pegmatites, high temperature hydrothermal
Black	Brown to Black	5.5	5.1	Pitchy luster	CHROMITE $FeCr_2O_4$	Mafic, magmatic segregation, placer

HARDNESS 2.5 to 5.5
(can be scratched with a knife)

searchable text view

Hardness: 3.5 to 4; **Specific Gravity:** 4.3
Name / Formula: CHALCOPYRITE / $CuFeS_2$
Geologic Environment: Medium temperature hydrothermal
Color: Brass-Yellow; **Streak:** Black
Remarks: Yellower than pyrite

Hardness: 4; **Specific Gravity:** 4.4
Name / Formula: MANGANITE / $MnO(OH)$
Geologic Environment: Low temperature hydrothermal
Color: Black; **Streak:** Gray to Black
Remarks: Sooty, fibrous

Hardness: 4; **Specific Gravity:** 4.6

Name / Formula: PYRRHOTITE / FeS
Geologic Environment: High temperature hydrothermal; mafic magmatic segregation
Color: Bronze; **Streak:** Black
Remarks: Slightly magnetic

Hardness: 4 to 4.5; **Specific Gravity:** 14-19
Name / Formula: PLATINUM / Pt
Geologic Environment: Mafic magmatic segregation; placer
Color: Silver-White; **Streak:** Gray
Remarks: Malleable

Hardness: 5 to 5.5; **Specific Gravity:** 3.5
Name / Formula: GOETHITE / FeO(OH)
Geologic Environment: Zone of oxidation
Color: Black to Gray; **Streak:** Yellow-Brown
Remarks: Botryoidal. Radiating crystals

Hardness: 5 to 6; **Specific Gravity:** 4.8
Name / Formula: ILMENITE / $FeTiO_3$
Geologic Environment: Mafic, magmatic segregation; high temperature hydrothermal, pegmatite, placer
Color: Black; **Streak:** Brown to Black
Remarks: Platy crystals, massive. Slightly magnetic

Hardness: 5 to 6; **Specific Gravity:** 8-11
Name / Formula: URANINITE / UO_2
Geologic Environment: Pegmatites, high temperature hydrothermal
Color: Black; **Streak:** Brown to Black
Remarks: Pitchy luster, massive, radioactive

Hardness: 5.5; **Specific Gravity:** 5.1
Name / Formula: CHROMITE / $FeCr_2O_4$
Geologic Environment: Mafic, magmatic segregation, placer
Color: Black; **Streak:** Brown to Black
Remarks: Pitchy luster

DETERMINATIVE TABLES
METALLIC or SUBMETALLIC LUSTER

HARDNESS Greater Than 5.5
(cannot be scratched with a knife)

DETERMINATIVE TABLES
METALLIC or SUBMETALLIC LUSTER

Color	Streak	Hardness	Sp. Gr.	Remarks	Name & Formula	Geologic Environment
HARDNESS Greater Than 5.5 (cannot be scratched with a knife)						
Tin-White	Black	5.5 to 6	6.0	Massive or granular. Associated with gold quartz. Dirty yellow stain	ARSENOPYRITE (Mispickel) FeAsS	Medium temperature hydrothermal
Gray to Black	Red Brown	5.5 to 6.5	5.0	Specularite	HEMATITE Fe_2O_3	Secondary iron
Black	Black	6	5.2	Strongly magnetic	MAGNETITE $FeFe_2O_4$	Mafic, magmatic segregation, contact metamorphic, placer
Pale Brass-Yellow	Black	6 to 6.5	5.0	Cubic and five-sided crystals	PYRITE FeS_2	Medium temperature hydrothermal
Pale Brass-Yellow	Black	6 to 6.5	4.9	Forms at lower temperature than pyrite. Cock's comb crystals, radiating masses	MARCASITE FeS_2	Low temperature hydrothermal

HARDNESS Greater Than 5.5
(cannot be scratched with a knife)

Hardness: 5.5 to 6; **Specific Gravity:** 6.0
Name / Formula: ARSENOPYRITE / (Mispickel) / FeAsS
Geologic Environment: Medium temperature hydrothermal
Color: Tin-White; **Streak:** Black
Remarks: Massive or granular. Associated with gold quartz. Dirty yellow stain

Hardness: 5.5 to 6.5; **Specific Gravity:** 5.0
Name / Formula: HEMATITE / Fe_2O_3

Geologic Environment: Secondary iron
Color: Gray to Black; **Streak:** Red Brown
Remarks: Specularite

Hardness: 6; **Specific Gravity:** 5.2
Name / Formula: MAGNETITE / $FeFe_2O_4$

Geologic Environment: Mafic, magmatic segregation, contact metamorphic, placer

Color: Black; **Streak:** Black
Remarks: Strongly magnetic

Hardness: 6 to 6.5; **Specific Gravity:** 5.0
Name / Formula: PYRITE / FeS_2

Geologic Environment: Medium temperature hydrothermal
Color: Pale Brass-Yellow; **Streak:** Black
Remarks: Cubic and five-sided crystals

Hardness: 6 to 6.5; **Specific Gravity:** 4.9
Name / Formula: MARCASITE / FeS_2

Geologic Environment: Low temperature hydrothermal
Color: Pale Brass-Yellow; **Streak:** Black
Remarks: Forms at lower temperature than pyrite. Cock's comb crystals, radiating masses

DETERMINATIVE TABLES
NON-METALLIC LUSTER

HARDNESS Less Than 2.5
(can be scratched with fingernail)

table view

A. Shows Good Cleavage

DETERMINATIVE TABLES
NON-METALLIC LUSTER

Color	Hardness	Sp. Gr.	Remarks	Name & Formula	Geologic Environment
			HARDNESS Less Than 2.5 (can be scratched with fingernail)		
			A. Shows Good Cleavage		
White to Dark Green	1	2.8	Greasy feel, soapstone	TALC $Mg_3Si_4O_{10}(OH)_2$	Medium grade regional meta-morphic; mafic igneous intrusive rocks.
Yellow-Brown	1 +	3.6 to 4.0	Earthy, yellow-brown streak	LIMONITE $FeO(OH)$	Oxide zone
Lemon Yellow	1.5 to 2	3.5	Resinous luster. Pale yellow streak	ORPIMENT As_2S_3	Low temperature hydrothermal
Colorless or White	2	2.0	Soluble in water. Bitter taste	SYLVITE KCl	Evaporite
Colorless or White	2	2.3	In crystals, fibrous or massive	GYPSUM $CaSO_4 \cdot 2H_2O$	Evaporite, caves
White	2 to 2.5	2.6	Claylike — will adhere to tongue	KAOLINITE $Al_2Si_2O_5(OH)_4$	Weathering of feldspars in igneous rock
Green	2 to 2.5	2.6-2.9	Flexible flakes	CHLORITE $(Mg,Fe,Al)_6(Si,Al)_4O_{10}(OH)_8$	Low-grade metamorphic; hydrothermal alteration
White	2 to 2.5	2.8-3.0	White mica	MUSCOVITE $KAl_2(Si_3Al)O_{10}(OH)_2$	Pegmatite and silicic intrusive igneous rock
Red	2 to 2.5	8.1	Adamantine luster	CINNABAR HgS	Low temperature hydrothermal
Colorless, White. Rarely Red/Blue	2 to 2.5	2.1-2.3	Cubic cleavage. Salty taste	HALITE $NaCl$	Evaporite

HARDNESS Less Than 2.5
(can be scratched with fingernail)

searchable text view

A. Shows Good Cleavage

Hardness: 1; **Specific Gravity:** 2.8
Name / Formula: TALC / $Mg_3Si_4O_{10}(OH)_2$
Geologic Environment: Medium grade regional meta-morphic; mafic igneous intrusive rocks.
Color: Color: White to Dark Green
Remarks: Greasy feel, soapstone

Hardness: 1 +; **Specific Gravity:** 3.6 to 4.0
Name / Formula: LIMONITE / $FeO(OH)$
Geologic Environment: Oxide zone
Color: Color: Yellow-Brown
Remarks: Earthy, yellow-brown streak

Hardness: 1.5 to 2; **Specific Gravity:** 3.5
Name / Formula: ORPIMENT / As_2S_3
Geologic Environment: Low temperature hydrothermal
Color: Lemon Yellow
Remarks: Resinous luster. Pale yellow streak

Hardness: 2; **Specific Gravity:** 2.0
Name / Formula: SYLVITE / KCl
Geologic Environment: Evaporite
Color: Colorless or White
Remarks: Soluble in water. Bitter taste

Hardness: 2; **Specific Gravity:** 2.3
Name / Formula: GYPSUM / $CaSO_4 \cdot 2H_2O$
Geologic Environment: Evaporite, caves
Color: Colorless or White
Remarks: In crystals, fibrous or massive

Hardness: 2 to 2.5; **Specific Gravity:** 2.6
Name / Formula: KAOLINITE / $Al_2Si_2O_5(OH)_4$
Geologic Environment: Weathering of feldspars in igneous rock
Color: White
Remarks: Claylike — will adhere to tongue

Hardness: 2 to 2.5; **Specific Gravity:** 2.6-2.9
Name / Formula: CHLORITE / $(Mg,Fe,Al)_6(Si,Al)_4O_{10}(OH)_8$
Geologic Environment: Low-grade metamorphic; hydrothermal alteration
Color: Green
Remarks: Flexible flakes

Hardness: 2 to 2.5; **Specific Gravity:** 2.8-3.0
Name / Formula: MUSCOVITE / $KAl_2(Si_3Al)O_{10}(OH)_2$
Geologic Environment: Pegmatite and silicic intrusive igneous rock
Color: White
Remarks: White mica

Hardness: 2 to 2.5; **Specific Gravity:** 8.1
 Name / Formula: CINNABAR / HgS
 Geologic Environment: Low temperature hydrothermal
 Color: Red
 Remarks: Adamantine luster

Hardness: 2 to 2.5; **Specific Gravity:** 2.1-2.3
 Name / Formula: HALITE / NaCl
 Geologic Environment: Evaporite
 Color: Colorless, White. Rarely Red/Blue
 Remarks: Cubic cleavage. Salty taste

DETERMINATIVE TABLES
NON-METALLIC LUSTER

HARDNESS Less Than 2.5
(can be scratched with fingernail)

table view

B. Shows No Cleavage

DETERMINATIVE TABLES
NON-METALLIC LUSTER

Color	Hardness	Sp. Gr.	Remarks	Name & Formula	Geologic Environment
			B. Shows No Cleavage		
Yellow, Brown, Gray, White	1 to 3	2.0-2.5	Earthy, may be in rounded grains	BAUXITE $AlO(OH)$	Residual
Deep Red to Orange	1.5 to 2	3.5	Earthy, commonly found with orpiment	REALGAR AsS	Low temperature hydrothermal
Pale Yellow	1.5 to 2.5	2.1		SULFUR S	Hot springs; evaporite
Gray	2 to 3	5.5	Horn silver, turns brown on exposure to light	CERARGYRITE $AgCl$	Low temperature hydrothermal
Green to Blue	2 to 4	2.0-2.4	Associated with copper mineralization. Vitreous luster	CHRYSOCOLLA $CuSiO_3 \cdot nH_2O$	Hydrothermal oxide zone

HARDNESS Less Than 2.5
(can be scratched with fingernail)

searchable text view

B. Shows No Cleavage

Hardness: 1 to 3; **Specific Gravity:** 2.0-2.5
Name / Formula: BAUXITE / $AlO(OH)$
Geologic Environment: Residual
Color: Yellow, Brown, Gray, White
Remarks: Earthy, may be in rounded grains

Hardness: 1.5 to 2; **Specific Gravity:** 3.5
Name / Formula: REALGAR / AsS
Geologic Environment: Low temperature hydrothermal
Color: Deep Red to Orange
Remarks: Earthy, commonly found with orpiment

Hardness: 1.5 to 2.5; **Specific Gravity:** 2.1
Name / Formula: SULFUR / S

Geologic Environment: Hot springs; evaporite
Color: Pale Yellow

Hardness: 2 to 3; **Specific Gravity:** 5.5
Name / Formula: CERARGYRITE / AgCl
Geologic Environment: Low temperature hydrothermal
Color: Gray
Remarks: Horn silver, turns brown on exposure to light

Hardness: 2 to 4; **Specific Gravity:** 2.0-2.4
Name / Formula: CHRYSOCOLLA / $CuSiO_3 \cdot nH_2O$

Geologic Environment: Hydrothermal oxide zone
Color: Green to Blue
Remarks: Associated with copper mineralization. Vitreous luster

DETERMINATIVE TABLES
NON-METALLIC LUSTER

HARDNESS Greater Than 2.5, Less Than 3
(can be scratched with a penny)

table view

DETERMINATIVE TABLES
NON-METALLIC LUSTER

Color	Hardness	Sp. Gr.	Remarks	Name & Formula	Geologic Environment
HARDNESS Greater Than 2.5, Less Than 3 (can be scratched with a penny)					
A. Shows Good Cleavage					
Dark Brown to Black	2.5 to 3	3.0	Black mica. Elastic flakes	BIOTITE $K(Fe,Mg)_2(Si_3Al)O_{10}(OH)_2$	Igneous rock
Yellow-Brown	2.5 to 3	2.9	May show copper-like reflection	PHLOGOPITE $K(Mg,Fe)_3(Si_3Al)O_{10}(OH)_2$	Medium to high-grade metamorphic; pegmatite
Lilac	2.5 to 4	2.8-3.0	Mica in small scales	LEPIDOLITE $K_2(Li,Al)_5(Si_6Al_2)O_{20}(OH,F)_4$	Pegmatite
Colorless, White tinted	3	2.7	Rhombohedral cleavage. Effervesces in acid	CALCITE $CaCO_3$	Low temperature hydrothermal; sedimentary; contact metamorphic
Colorless, White Tinted; Gray and Brown when impure	3	6.2-6.4	Adamantine luster. Massive tabular crystals	ANGLESITE $PbSO_4$	Hydrothermal oxide zone
B. Shows No Cleavage					
Dark, Green, Yellow, Green	2.5 to 3	2.2	Massive. Feels greasy. Fibrous variety called CHRYSOTILE (asbestos)	SERPENTINE $Mg_3Si_2O_5(OH)_4$	Low-grade metamorphic

HARDNESS Greater Than 2.5, Less Than 3
(can be scratched with a penny)

searchable text view

A. Shows Good Cleavage

Hardness: 2.5 to 3; **Specific Gravity:** 3.0
Name / Formula: BIOTITE / $K(Fe,Mg)_2(Si_3Al)O_{10}(OH)_2$

Geologic Environment: Igneous rock
Color: Dark Brown to Black
Remarks: Black mica. Elastic flakes

Hardness: 2.5 to 3; **Specific Gravity:** 2.9
Name / Formula: PHLOGOPITE / $K(Mg,Fe)_3(Si_3Al)O_{10}(OH)_2$

Geologic Environment: Medium to high-grade metamorphic; pegmatite
Color: Yellow-Brown
Remarks: May show copper-like reflection

Hardness: 2.5 to 4; **Specific Gravity:** 2.8-3.0
Name / Formula: LEPIDOLITE / $K_2(Li,Al)_5(Si_6Al_2)O_{20}(OH,F)_4$

Geologic Environment: Pegmatite
Color: Lilac
Remarks: Mica in small scales

Hardness: 3; **Specific Gravity:** 2.7
Name / Formula: CALCITE / $CaCO_3$

Geologic Environment: Low temperature hydrothermal; sedimentary; contact metamorphic
Color: Colorless,
White tinted
Remarks: Rhombohedral cleavage. Effervesces in acid

Hardness: 3; **Specific Gravity:** 6.2-6.4
Name / Formula: ANGLESITE / $PbSO_4$

Geologic Environment: Hydrothermal oxide zone
Color: Colorless, White Tinted; Gray and Brown when impure
Remarks: Admantine luster.
Massive tabular crystals

B. Shows No Cleavage

Hardness: 2.5 to 3; **Specific Gravity:** 2.2
Name / Formula: SERPENTINE / $Mg_3Si_2O_5(OH)_4$

Geologic Environment: Low-grade metamorphic
Color: Dark, Green, Yellow, Green
Remarks: Massive. Feels greasy. Fibrous variety called CHRYSOTILE (asbestos)

DETERMINATIVE TABLES
NON-METALLIC LUSTER

HARDNESS Greater Than 3, Less Than 5.5
(will scratch with a knife blade)

table view

A. Shows Good Cleavage

DETERMINATIVE TABLES
NON-METALLIC LUSTER

Color	Hardness	Sp. Gr.	Remarks	Name & Formula	Geologic Environment
HARDNESS Greater Than 3, Less Than 5.5 (will scratch with a knife blade)					
A. Shows Good Cleavage					
Colorless, Blue, White, Gray	3 to 3.5	2.9-3.0	Three cleavages at right angles, usually massive	ANHYDRITE $CaSO_4$	Evaporite
Colorless, Red, White, Blue	3 to 3.5	4.0	Three cleavages	CELESTITE $SrSO_4$	Low temperature hydrothermal; evaporite
Colorless, White, Blue, Yellow	3 to 3.5	4.5	Three cleavages, pearly luster. Platy aggregates; red-brown barite rose	BARITE $BaSO_4$	Medium to low temperature hydrothermal
Colorless, White, Brown.	3 to 3.5	6.6	Long tabular crystals	CERUSSITE $PbCO_3$	Oxide zone of hydrothermal lead deposits
Colorless, White	3.5	4.3		WITHERITE $BaCO_3$	Low temperature hydrothermal
White, Yellow, Brown, Red	3.5 to 4	2.1-2.2	Zeolite. Fills vesicles in basalt	STILBITE $NaCa_2(Al_5Si_{13})O_{36} \cdot 14H_2O$	Volcanic
White, Yellow, Red, Orange	3.5 to 4	2.2	Zeolite. Tabular crystals, pearly luster	HEULANDITE $(Na,Ca)_4Al_6(Al,Si)_4Si_{26}O_{72} \cdot 24H_2O$	Volcanic

HARDNESS Greater Than 3, Less Than 5.5
(will scratch with a knife blade)

searchable text view

A. Shows Good Cleavage

Hardness: 3 to 3.5; **Specific Gravity:** 2.9-3.0
Name / Formula: ANHYDRITE / $CaSO_4$
Geologic Environment: Evaporite
Color: Colorless, Blue, White, Gray
Remarks: Three cleavages at right angles, usually massive

Hardness: 3 to 3.5; **Specific Gravity:** 4.0
Name / Formula: CELESTITE / $SrSO_4$
Geologic Environment: Low temperature hydrothermal; evaporite
Color: Colorless, Red, White, Blue

Remarks: Three cleavages

Hardness: 3 to 3.5; **Specific Gravity:** 4.5
Name / Formula: BARITE / $BaSO_4$

Geologic Environment: Medium to low temperature hydrothermal
Color: Colorless, White, Blue, Yellow
Remarks: Three cleavages, pearly luster. Platy aggregates; red-brown barite rose

Hardness: 3 to 3.5; **Specific Gravity:** 6.6
Name / Formula: CERUSSITE / $PbCO_3$

Geologic Environment: Oxide zone of hydrothermal lead deposits
Color: Colorless, White, Brown,
Remarks: Long tabular crystals

Hardness: 3.5; **Specific Gravity:** 4.3
Name / Formula: WITHERITE / $BaCO_3$

Geologic Environment: Low temperature hydrothermal
Color: Colorless, White

Hardness: 3.5 to 4; **Specific Gravity:** 2.1-2.2
Name / Formula: STILBITE / $NaCa_2(Al_5Si_{13})O_{36} \cdot 14H_2O$

Geologic Environment: Volcanic
Color: White, Yellow, Brown, Red
Remarks: Zeolite. Fills vesicles in basalt

Hardness: 3.5 to 4; **Specific Gravity:** 2.2
Name / Formula: HEULANDITE / $(Na,Ca)_4Al_6(Al,Si)_4Si_{26}O_{72} \cdot 24H_2O$

Geologic Environment: Volcanic
Color: White, Yellow, Red, Orange
Remarks: Zeolite. Tabular crystals, pearly luster

DETERMINATIVE TABLES
NON-METALLIC LUSTER

HARDNESS Greater Than 3, Less Than 5.5
(will scratch with a knife blade)

table view

A. Shows Good Cleavage

DETERMINATIVE TABLES
NON-METALLIC LUSTER

Color	Hardness	Sp. Gr.	Remarks	Name & Formula	Geologic Environment
Colorless, White, Pink	3.5 to 4	2.8	Pearly luster. Curved rhombohedral crystals	DOLOMITE $CaMg(CO_3)_2$	Sedimentary; low temperature hydrothermal; metamorphic
Colorless, White	3.5 to 4	3.0	Strong effervescence in acid	ARAGONITE $CaCO_3$	Medium-grade metamorphic; sedimentary; hot springs
Light to Dark Brown	3.5 to 4	3.8-3.9	Rhombohedral cleavage	SIDERITE $FeCO_3$	Medium to low temperature hydrothermal
Yellow, Brown, Black, Red	3.5 to 4	3.9-4.1	Resinous luster; red with no iron; darker with iron ("blackjack")	SPHALERITE $(Zn,Fe)S$	Medium temperature hydrothermal
Pink	3.5 to 4.5	3.5-3.6	Rhombohedral cleavage	RHODOCHROSITE $MnCO_3$	Medium temperature hydrothermal
White, Yellow, Gray, Brown	3.5 to 5	3.0-3.2	Dense compact masses or cleavable aggregates	MAGNESITE $MgCO_3$	Ultramafic igneous rocks; hydrothermal
Colorless, Violet, Green, Yellow, Brown	4	3.2	Cubic crystals. Octahedral cleavage	FLUORITE CaF_2	Medium to high temperature hydrothermal; pegmatite

HARDNESS Greater Than 3, Less Than 5.5
(will scratch with a knife blade)

searchable text view

A. Shows Good Cleavage

Hardness: 3.5 to 4; **Specific Gravity:** 2.8
Name / Formula: DOLOMITE / $CaMg(CO_3)_2$

Geologic Environment: Sedimentary; low temperature hydrothermal; metamorphic
Color: Colorless, White, Pink
Remarks: Pearly luster. Curved rhombohedral crystals

Hardness: 3.5 to 4; **Specific Gravity:** 3.0
Name / Formula: ARAGONITE / $CaCO_3$

Geologic Environment: Medium-grade metamorphic; sedimentary; hot springs
Color: Colorless, White

Remarks: Strong effervescence in acid

Hardness: 3.5 to 4; **Specific Gravity:** 3.8-3.9
Name / Formula: SIDERITE / $FeCO_3$
Geologic Environment: Medium to low temperature hydrothermal
Color: Light to Dark Brown
Remarks: Rhombohedral cleavage

Hardness: 3.5 to 4; **Specific Gravity:** 3.9-4.1
Name / Formula: SPHALERITE / $(Zn,Fe)S$
Geologic Environment: Medium temperature hydrothermal
Color: Yellow, Brown, Black, Red
Remarks: Resinous luster; red with no iron; darker with iron ("blackjack")

Hardness: 3.5 to 4.5; **Specific Gravity:** 3.5-3.6
Name / Formula: RHODOCHROSITE / $MnCO_3$
Geologic Environment: Medium temperature hydrothermal
Color: Pink
Remarks: Rhombohedral cleavage

Hardness: 3.5 to 5; **Specific Gravity:** 3.0-3.2
Name / Formula: MAGNESITE / $MgCO_3$
Geologic Environment: Ultramafic igneous rocks; hydrothermal
Color: White, Yellow, Gray, Brown
Remarks: Dense compact masses or cleavable aggregates

Hardness: 4; **Specific Gravity:** 3.2
Name / Formula: FLUORITE / CaF_2
Geologic Environment: Medium to high temperature hydrothermal; pegmatite
Color: Colorless, Violet, Green, Yellow, Brown
Remarks: Cubic crystals.
Octahedral cleavage

DETERMINATIVE TABLES
NON-METALLIC LUSTER

HARDNESS Greater Than 3, Less Than 5.5
(will scratch with a knife blade)

A. Shows Good Cleavage

DETERMINATIVE TABLES
NON-METALLIC LUSTER

Color	Hardness	Sp. Gr.	Remarks	Name & Formula	Geologic Environment
White, Yellow, Red	4.5	2.1-2.2	Zeolite. Rhombohedral crystals; fills vesicles in basalt	CHABAZITE $CaAl_2Si_4O_{12} \cdot 6H_2O$	Volcanic
Blue, White, Gray, Green	5 to 7	3.6-3.7	Bladed aggregates. Hardness 5 parallel to length; 7 across	KYANITE Al_2OSiO_4	High-grade regional metamorphic
Colorless, White	5 to 5.5	2.2	Zeolite. Slender prismatic crystals, radiating groups. Fills vesicles in basalt	NATROLITE $Na_2(Al_2Si_3)O_{10} \cdot 2H_2O$	Volcanic
Colorless, White, Gray	5 to 5.5	2.8-2.9	Usually cleavable masses	WOLLASTONITE $CaSiO_3$	Low-grade regional and contact metamorphic
White, Green, Black	5 to 6	3.0-3.3	Crystals tabular and slender; two cleavage directions at 55°	AMPHIBOLE GROUP (Hornblende) $(Ca,Na,K)_2(Mg,Fe,Al)_5(Si,Al)_8O_{22}(OH,F)_2$	Igneous, medium-grade regional metamorphic
White, Green, Black	5 to 6	3.1-3.5	Crystals tabular and short and stout. Two cleavages at nearly 90°	PYROXENE GROUP $(Ca,Mg,Fe,Ti,Al)_2(Si,Al)_2O_6$	Mafic and ultramafic igneous medium-grade regional metamorphic
Brown, Green, Bronze, Black	5.5	3.2-3.5	Prismatic crystals, fibrous and massive	ENSTATITE $MgSiO_3$	Basic and ultrabasic igneous; high-grade regional metamorphic

HARDNESS Greater Than 3, Less Than 5.5
(will scratch with a knife blade)

A. Shows Good Cleavage

Hardness: 4.5; **Specific Gravity:** 2.1-2.2
Name / Formula: CHABAZITE / $CaAl_2Si_4O_{12} \cdot 6H_2O$

Geologic Environment: Volcanic
Color: White, Yellow, Red
Remarks: Zeolite. Rhombohedral crystals; fills vesicles in basalt

Hardness: 5 to 7; **Specific Gravity:** 3.6-3.7
Name / Formula: KYANITE / Al_2OSiO_4

Geologic Environment: High-grade regional metamorphic
Color: Blue, White, Gray, Green

Remarks: Bladed aggregates. Hardness 5 parallel to length; 7 across

Hardness: 5 to 5.5; **Specific Gravity:** 2.2
Name / Formula: NATROLITE / $Na_2(Al_2Si_3)O_{10} \cdot 2H_2O$

Geologic Environment: Volcanic
Color: Colorless, White
Remarks: Zeolite. Slender prismatic crystals, radiating groups.
Fills vesicles in basalt

Hardness: 5 to 5.5; **Specific Gravity:** 2.8-2.9
Name / Formula: WOLLASTONITE / $CaSiO_3$

Geologic Environment: Low-grade regional and contact metamorphic
Color: Colorless, White, Gray
Remarks: Usually cleavable masses

Hardness: 5 to 6; **Specific Gravity:** 3.0-3.3
Name / Formula: AMPHIBOLE GROUP (Hornblende)
$(Ca,Na,K)_2(Mg,Fe,Al)_5(Si,Al)_8O_{22}(OH,F)_2$

Geologic Environment: Igneous, medium-grade regional metamorphic
Color: White, Green,
Black
Remarks: Crystals tabular and slender; two cleavage directions at 55°

Hardness: 5 to 6; **Specific Gravity:** 3.1-3.5
Name / Formula: PYROXENE GROUP / $(Ca,Mg,Fe,Ti,Al)_2(Si,Al)_2O_6$

Geologic Environment: Mafic and ultramafic igneous medium-grade regional
metamorphic
Color: White, Green Black
Remarks: Crystals tabular and short and stout. Two cleavages at nearly 90°

Hardness: 5.5; **Specific Gravity:** 3.2-3.5
Name / Formula: ENSTATITE / $MgSiO_3$

Geologic Environment: Basic and ultrabasic igneous;
high-grade regional metamorphic
Color: Brown, Green,
Bronze, Black
Remarks: Prismatic crystals, fibrous and massive

DETERMINATIVE TABLES
NON-METALLIC LUSTER

HARDNESS Greater Than 3, Less Than 5.5
(will scratch with a knife blade)

table view

B. Shows No Cleavage

DETERMINATIVE TABLES
NON-METALLIC LUSTER

Color	Hardness	Sp. Gr.	Remarks	Name & Formula	Geologic Environment
			B. Shows No Cleavage		
Colorless, White	3.5	4.3	Radiating masses	WITHERITE $BaCO_3$	Low temperature hydrothermal
Colorless, White	3.5 to 4	3.7	Prismatic crystals, massive	STRONTIANITE $SrCO_3$	Low temperature hydrothermal
Blue	3.5 to 4	3.8	Azure blue, found with malachite	AZURITE $Cu_3(CO_3)_2(OH)_2$	Oxide zone of hydrothermal copper deposits
Bright Green	3.5 to 4	3.9-4.0	Mammillary, fibrous. Found with azurite	MALACHITE $Cu_2CO_3(OH)_2$	Oxide zone of hydrothermal copper deposits
Red	3.5 to 4	6.0	Massive or cubic crystals. Red streak	CUPRITE Cu_2O	Oxide zone of hydrothermal copper deposits
Green, Brown, Yellow, Gray	3.5 to 4	6.5-7.1	Hexagonal crystals, often cavernous	PYROMORPHITE $Pb_5(PO_4,AsO_4)_3Cl$	Oxide zone of hydrothermal lead deposits
Colorless, White	3.5 to 4	3.0-3.2	Dense compact masses	MAGNESITE $MgCO_3$	Alteration of ultramafic rocks; hydrothermal
White, Grayish, Red	4	2.6-2.8	Massive	ALUNITE $KAl_3(SO_4)_2(OH)_6$	Silicic igneous rock alteration

HARDNESS Greater Than 3, Less Than 5.5
(will scratch with a knife blade)

searchable text view

B. Shows No Cleavage

Hardness: 3.5; **Specific Gravity:** 4.3
Name / Formula: WITHERITE / $BaCO_3$

Geologic Environment: Low temperature hydrothermal
Color: Colorless, White
Remarks: Radiating masses

Hardness: 3.5 to 4; **Specific Gravity:** 3.7
Name / Formula: STRONTIANITE / $SrCO_3$

Geologic Environment: Low temperature hydrothermal
Color: Colorless, White

Remarks: Prismatic crystals, massive

Hardness: 3.5 to 4; **Specific Gravity:** 3.8
Name / Formula: AZURITE / $Cu_3(CO_3)_2(OH)_2$

Geologic Environment: Oxide zone of hydrothermal copper deposits
Color: Blue
Remarks: Azure blue, found with malachite

Hardness: 3.5 to 4; **Specific Gravity:** 3.9-4.0
Name / Formula: MALACHITE / $Cu_2CO_3(OH)_2$

Geologic Environment: Oxide zone of hydrothermal copper deposits
Color: Bright Green
Remarks: Mammillary, fibrous.
Found with azurite

Hardness: 3.5 to 4; **Specific Gravity:** 6.0
Name / Formula: CUPRITE / Cu_2O

Geologic Environment: Oxide zone of hydrothermal copper deposits
Color: Red
Remarks: Massive or cubic crystals.
Red streak

Hardness: 3.5 to 4; **Specific Gravity:** 6.5-7.1
Name / Formula: PYROMORPHITE / $Pb_5(PO_4,AsO_4)_3Cl$

Geologic Environment: Oxide zone of hydrothermal lead deposits
Color: Green, Brown, Yellow, Gray
Remarks: Hexagonal crystals, often cavernous

Hardness: 3.5 to 4; **Specific Gravity:** 3.0-3.2
Name / Formula: MAGNESITE / $MgCO_3$

Geologic Environment: Alteration of ultramafic rocks; hydrothermal
Color: Colorless, White
Remarks: Dense compact masses

Hardness: 4; **Specific Gravity:** 2.6-2.8
Name / Formula: ALUNITE / $KAl_3(SO_4)_2(OH)_6$

Geologic Environment: Silicic igneous rock alteration
Color: White, Grayish, Red
Remarks: Massive

DETERMINATIVE TABLES
NON-METALLIC LUSTER

HARDNESS Greater Than 3, Less Than 5.5
(will scratch with a knife blade)

table view

B. Shows No Cleavage

DETERMINATIVE TABLES
NON-METALLIC LUSTER

Color	Hardness	Sp. Gr.	Remarks	Name & Formula	Geologic Environment
White, Green, Blue	4.5 to 5	3.4-3.5	Radiating crystal groups	HEMIMORPHITE $Zn_4Si_2O_7(OH)_2 \cdot H_2O$	Oxide zone of hydrothermal lead and zinc deposits
White, Yellow, Brown	4.5 to 5	5.9-6.1	Adamantine to vitreous luster; tabular crystals. Fluorescent-tight blue	SCHEELITE $Ca(WO_4,MoO_4)$	Contact metamorphic, high temperature hydrothermal
Green, Blue, Brown, Violet	5	3.2	Hexagonal prisms; massive	APATITE $Ca_5(PO_4)_3(OH,F,Cl)$	Igneous, sedimentary, metamorphic
Colorless, White	5 to 5.5	2.3	Feldspathoid. Fills vesicles in basalts	ANALCIME (Analcite) $NaAlSi_2O_6 \cdot 2H_2O$	Volcanic
Colorless, Pale Green, Yellow	5 to 5.5	2.8-3.0	Brilliant cyrstals associated with zeolites. Fills vesicles in basalts	DATOLITE $CaBSiO_4(OH)$	Volcanic
Black	5 to 6	3.7-4.7	Botryoidal, massive	PSILOMELANE $BaMnMn_8O_{16}(OH)_4$	Hydrothermal oxide zone; sedimentary
Any color	5 to 6.5	1.9-2.2	Greasy luster; conchoidal fracture	OPAL $SiO_2 \cdot nH_2O$	Hot springs and volcanic

HARDNESS Greater Than 3, Less Than 5.5
(will scratch with a knife blade)

searchable text view

B. Shows No Cleavage

Hardness: 4.5 to 5; **Specific Gravity:** 3.4-3.5
Name / Formula: HEMIMORPHITE / $Zn_4Si_2O_7(OH)_2 \cdot H_2O$
Geologic Environment: Oxide zone of hydrothermal lead and zinc deposits
Color: White, Green, Blue
Remarks: Radiating crystal groups

Hardness: 4.5 to 5; **Specific Gravity:** 5.9-6.1
Name / Formula: SCHEELITE / $Ca(WO_4,MoO_4)$
Geologic Environment: Contact metamorphic, high temperature hydrothermal
Color: White, Yellow, Brown

Remarks: Adamantine to vitreous luster; tabular crystals. Fluorescent-tight blue

Hardness: 5; **Specific Gravity:** 3.2
Name / Formula: APATITE / $Ca_5(PO_4)_3(OH,F,Cl)$

Geologic Environment: Igneous, sedimentary, metamorphic
Color: Green, Blue, Brown, Violet
Remarks: Hexagonal prisms; massive

Hardness: 5 to 5.5; **Specific Gravity:** 2.3
Name / Formula: ANALCIME (Analcite) / $NaAlSi_2O_6 \cdot 2H_2O$

Geologic Environment: Volcanic
Color: Colorless, White
Remarks: Feldspathoid. Fills vesicles in basalts

Hardness: 5 to 5.5; **Specific Gravity:** 2.8-3.0
Name / Formula: DATOLITE / $CaBSiO_4(OH)$

Geologic Environment: Volcanic
Color: Colorless, Pale Green, Yellow
Remarks: Brilliant cyrstals associated with zeolites. Fills vesicles in basalts

Hardness: 5 to 6; **Specific Gravity:** 3.7-4.7
Name / Formula: PSILOMELANE / $BaMnMn_8O_{16}(OH)_4$

Geologic Environment: Hydrothermal oxide zone; sedimentary
Color: Black
Remarks: Botryoidal, massive

Hardness: 5 to 6.5; **Specific Gravity:** 1.9-2.2
Name / Formula: OPAL / $SiO_2 \cdot nH_2O$

Geologic Environment: Hot springs and volcanic
Color: Any color
Remarks: Greasy luster; conchoidal fracture

DETERMINATIVE TABLES
NON-METALLIC LUSTER

HARDNESS Greater Than 5-1/2, Less Than 7

table view

A. Shows Good Cleavage

DETERMINATIVE TABLES
NON-METALLIC LUSTER

Color	Hardness	Sp. Gr.	Remarks	Name & Formula	Geologic Environment
			HARDNESS Greater Than 5-1/2, Less Than 7		
			A. Shows Good Cleavage		
Red, Pink	5.5 to 6	3.6-3.7	Massive; two cleavages at nearly 90°	RHODONITE (Mn,Fe,Mg)SiO$_3$	Contact metamorphic
White, Gray, Pink, Green	6	2.5	Tabular crystals and irregular grains	ORTHOCLASE MICROCLINE ADULARIA KAlSi$_3$O$_8$	Silicic to intermediate igneous; arkose; metamorphic
Colorless, White, Gray	6	2.6-2.8	Tabular crystals and irregular grains	PLAGIOCLASE (Na,Ca)(Al,Si)$_4$O$_8$	Igneous and metamorphic
White, Green, Blue	6	3.0-3.1	Cleavable masses resembling feldspar	AMBLYGONITE (Li,Na)Al(PO$_4$)(F,OH)	Pegmatite
Grayish, Green, Brown	6 to 7	3.2	Long slender crystals in schists	SILLIMANITE Al$_2$OSiO$_4$	High-grade regional metamorphic and contact metamorphic
Yellowish to Green-Black	6 to 7	3.3-3.4	Massive or crusts	EPIDOTE Ca$_2$Fe(Al$_2$O)(OH)(Si$_2$O$_7$)(SiO$_4$)	Medium-grade regional metamorphic, contact metamorphic
White, Gray, Pink, Green	6.5 to 7	3.1-3.2	Flattened striated crystals	SPODUMENE LiAl(SiO$_3$)$_2$	Pegmatite
Green, Gray, White	6.5 to 7	3.3-3.5	Massive, compact. Difficult to break	JADEITE - NEPHRITE NaAl(SiO$_3$)$_2$	Medium-grade regional metamorphic
Blue, Gray	7	3.6	Bladed aggregates. Hardness 5 parallel to length; 7 across	KYANITE Al$_2$OSiO$_4$	High-grade regional metamorphic

HARDNESS Greater Than 5-1/2, Less Than 7

searchable text view

A. Shows Good Cleavage

Hardness: 5.5 to 6; **Specific Gravity:** 3.6-3.7
Name / Formula: RHODONITE / (Mn,Fe,Mg)SiO$_3$

Geologic Environment: Contact metamorphic
Color: Red, Pink
Remarks: Massive; two cleavages at nearly 90°

Hardness: 6; **Specific Gravity:** 2.5
Name / Formula: ORTHOCLASE / MICROCLINE / ADULARIA / KAlSi$_3$O$_8$
Geologic Environment: Silicic to intermediate igneous; arkose; metamorphic

Color: White, Gray, Pink, Green
Remarks: Tabular crystals and irregular grains

Hardness: 6; **Specific Gravity:** 2.6-2.8
Name / Formula: PLAGIOCLASE / $(Na,Ca)(Al,Si)_4O_8$

Geologic Environment: Igneous and metamorphic
Color: Colorless, White, Gray
Remarks: Tabular crystals and irregular grains

Hardness: 6; **Specific Gravity:** 3.0-3.1
Name / Formula: AMBLYGONITE / $(Li,Na)Al(PO_4)(F,OH)$

Geologic Environment: Pegmatite
Color: White, Green, Blue
Remarks: Cleavable masses resembling feldspar

Hardness: 6 to 7; **Specific Gravity:** 3.2
Name / Formula: SILLIMANITE / Al_2OSiO_4

Geologic Environment: High-grade regional metamorphic and contact metamorphic
Color: Grayish, Green, Brown
Remarks: Long slender crystals in schists

Hardness: 6 to 7; **Specific Gravity:** 3.3-3.4
Name / Formula: EPIDOTE / $Ca_2Fe(Al_2O)(OH)(Si_2O_7)(SiO_4)$

Geologic Environment: Medium-grade regional metamorphic, contact metamorphic
Color: Yellowish to Green-Black
Remarks: Massive or crusts

Hardness: 6.5to 7; **Specific Gravity:** 3.1-3.2
Name / Formula: SPODUMENE / $LiAl(SiO_3)_2$

Geologic Environment: Pegmatite
Color: White, Gray, Pink, Green
Remarks: Flattened striated crystals

Hardness: 6.5 to 7; **Specific Gravity:** 3.3-3.5
Name / Formula: JADEITE - NEPHRITE / $NaAl(SiO_3)_2$

Geologic Environment: Medium-grade regional metamorphic
Color: Green, Gray, White
Remarks: Massive, compact. Difficult to break

Hardness: 7; **Specific Gravity:** 3.6

Name / Formula: KYANITE / Al_2OSiO_4

Geologic Environment: High-grade regional metamorphic

Color: Blue, Gray

Remarks: Bladed aggregates. Hardness 5 parallel to length; 7 across

B. Shows No Cleavage

DETERMINATIVE TABLES
NON-METALLIC LUSTER

Color	Hardness	Sp. Gr.	Remarks	Name & Formula	Geologic Environment
			B. Shows No Cleavage		
Any color	5 to 6.5	1.9-2.2	Conchoidal fracture	OPAL $SiO_2 \cdot nH_2O$	Circulating silica-rich ground water
Brown, Green, Blue, White	5.5	4.3-4.4	Botryoidal masses	SMITHSONITE $ZnCO_3$	Oxide zone of hydrothermal deposits
Blue, Green, White, Gray	5.5 to 6	2.1-2.3	Massive or embedded grains. Not found with quartz	SODALITE $Na_8(Al_6Si_6O_{24})Cl_2$	Silica-poor silicic igneous
Gray, White, Colorless	5.5 to 6	2.4-2.5	Crystals embedded in dark igneous rocks	LEUCITE $KAlSi_2O_6$	Silica-poor dark igneous
White, Gray, Greenish, Red	5.5 to 6	2.5-2.6	Greasy luster. Not found with quartz	NEPHELINE $Na_3KAl_4Si_4O_{16}$	Silica-poor silicic igneous
Gray	5.5 to 6.5	5.2	Specularite variety. Red-brown streak	HEMATITE Fe_2O_3	Oxide zone of hydrothermal deposits
Blue, Bluish Green, Green	6	2.6-2.8	Blebs and veinlets	TURQUOISE $CuAl_6(PO_4)(OH)_8$	Oxide zone copper deposits
Green, Gray, White	6 to 6.5	2.8-2.9	Associated with zeolite minerals	PREHNITE $Ca_2Al(AlSi_3)O_{10}(OH)_2$	Volcanic

HARDNESS Greater Than 5-1/2, Less Than 7

searchable text view

B. Shows No Cleavage

Hardness: 5 to 6.5; **Specific Gravity:** 1.9-2.2
Name / Formula: OPAL / $SiO_2 \cdot nH_2O$

Geologic Environment: Circulating silica-rich ground water
Color: Any color
Remarks: Conchoidal fracture

Hardness: 5.5; **Specific Gravity:** 4.3-4.4
Name / Formula: SMITHSONITE / $ZnCO_3$

Geologic Environment: Oxide zone of hydrothermal deposits
Color: Brown, Green, Blue, White
Remarks: Botryoidal masses

Hardness: 5.5 to 6; **Specific Gravity:** 2.1-2.3

Name / Formula: SODALITE / $Na_8(Al_6Si_6O_{24})Cl_2$

Geologic Environment: Silica-poor silicic igneous

Color: Blue, Green, White, Gray

Remarks: Massive or embedded grains. Not found with quartz

Hardness: 5.5 to 6; **Specific Gravity:** 2.4-2.5

Name / Formula: LEUCITE / $KAlSi_2O_6$

Geologic Environment: Silica-poor dark igneous

Color: Gray, White, Colorless

Remarks: Crystals embedded in dark igneous rocks

Hardness: 5.5 to 6; **Specific Gravity:** 2.5-2.6

Name / Formula: NEPHELINE / $Na_3KAl_4Si_4O_{16}$

Geologic Environment: Silica-poor silicic igneous

Color: White, Gray, Greenish, Red

Remarks: Greasy luster. Not found with quartz

Hardness: 5.5 to 6.5; **Specific Gravity:** 5.2

Name / Formula: HEMATITE / Fe_2O_3

Geologic Environment: Oxide zone of hydrothermal deposits

Color: Gray

Remarks: Specularite variety. Red-brown streak

Hardness: 6; **Specific Gravity:** 2.6-2.8

Name / Formula: TURQUOISE / $CuAl_6(PO_4)(OH)_8$

Geologic Environment: Oxide zone copper deposits

Color: Blue, Bluish Green, Green

Remarks: Blebs and veinlets

Hardness: 6 to 6.5; **Specific Gravity:** 2.8-2.9

Name / Formula: PREHNITE / $Ca_2Al(AlSi_3)O_{10}(OH)_2$

Geologic Environment: Volcanic

Color: Green, Gray, White

Remarks: Associated with zeolite minerals

DETERMINATIVE TABLES
NON-METALLIC LUSTER

HARDNESS Greater Than 5-1/2, Less Than 7

table view

B. Shows No Cleavage

DETERMINATIVE TABLES
NON-METALLIC LUSTER

Color	Hardness	Sp. Gr.	Remarks	Name & Formula	Geologic Environment
Reddish Brown to Black	6 to 6.5	2.2	Vertically striated crystals	RUTILE TiO_2	Igneous and metamorphic rocks, placer
Brown to Black	6 to 7	6.8-7.1	Reniform surface	CASSITERITE SnO_2	Granitic rocks; high temperature hydrothermal placer
Green, Brown	6.5 to 7	3.3	Disseminated grains. Not found with quartz	OLIVINE $(Mg,Fe)_2SiO_4$	Mafic igneous
Brown, Red, Yellow, Green	6.5 to 7.5	3.5-4.3	Six varieties of GARNET:	SPESSARTITE, PYROPE, ALMANDINE, GROSSULAR (GROSSULARITE), UVAROVITE and ANDRADITE $(Fe,Ca,Mg,Mn)_3(Al,Fe,Cr)_2Si_3O_{12}$	Mafic intrusive igneous rocks; regional contact metamorphic placer
Colorless, White, Variously Colored	7	2.7	Six-sided crystals with horizontal striations	QUARTZ SiO_2	Igneous; sedimentary and metamorphic hydrothermal veins
Many Colors	7	2.7	Veins, geodes, crusts, agate when banded	CHALCEDONY SiO_2	Fills fractures in rocks
Any Color	7	2.7	Veinlets, opaque, brown, yellow, green variety termed jasper	CHERT SiO_2	Fracture filling; sedimentary nodules

HARDNESS Greater Than 5-1/2, Less Than 7

searchable text view

B. Shows No Cleavage

Hardness: 6 to 6.5; **Specific Gravity:** 2.2
Name / Formula: RUTILE / TiO_2

Geologic Environment: Igneous and metamorphic rocks, placer
Color: Reddish Brown to Black
Remarks: Vertically striated crystals

Hardness: 6 to 7; **Specific Gravity:** 6.8-7.1
Name / Formula: CASSITERITE / SnO_2

Geologic Environment: Granitic rocks; high temperature hydrothermal placer
Color: Brown to Black
Remarks: Reniform surface

Hardness: 6.5 to 7; **Specific Gravity:** 3.3

Name / Formula: OLIVINE / $(Mg,Fe)_2SiO_4$
Geologic Environment: Mafic igneous
Color: Green, Brown
Remarks: Disseminated grains. Not found with quartz

Hardness: 6.5 to 7.5; **Specific Gravity:** 3.5-4.3
Name / Formula: GARNET varieties - SPESSARTITE, PYROPE, ALMANDINE, GROSSULAR (GROSSULARITE), UVAROVITE and ANDRADITE / $(Fe,Ca,Mg,Mn)_3(Al,Fe,Cr)_2Si_3O_{12}$
Geologic Environment: Mafic intrusive igneous rocks; regional contact metamorphic placer
Color: Brown, Red, Yellow, Green
Remarks: Six varieties of GARNET:

Hardness: 7; **Specific Gravity:** 2.7
Name / Formula: QUARTZ / SiO_2
Geologic Environment: Igneous; sedimentary and metamorphic hydrothermal veins
Color: Colorless, White, Variously Colored
Remarks: Six-sided crystals with horizontal striations

Hardness: 7; **Specific Gravity:** 2.7
Name / Formula: CHALCEDONY / SiO_2
Geologic Environment: Fills fractures in rocks
Color: Many Colors
Remarks: Veins, geodes, crusts, agate when banded

Hardness: 7; **Specific Gravity:** 2.7
Name / Formula: CHERT / SiO_2
Geologic Environment: Fracture filling; sedimentary nodules
Color: Any Color
Remarks: Veinlets, opaque, brown, yellow, green variety termed jasper

DETERMINATIVE TABLES
NON-METALLIC LUSTER
HARDNESS Greater Than 7

table view

DETERMINATIVE TABLES
NON-METALLIC LUSTER

Color	Hardness	Sp. Gr.	Remarks	Name & Formula	Geologic Environment
			HARDNESS Greater Than 7		
			A. Shows Good Cleavage		
Blue, Colorless	7 to 7.5	2.6	Embedded grains resembling quartz	CORDIERITE $Mg_2Al_4Si_5O_{18}$	Contact metamorphic rocks. Low-grade regional metamorphic rocks
Colorless, Yellow, Pink, Blue, Green	8	3.4-3.6	Usually in crystals	TOPAZ $Al_2(SiO_4)(OH,F)_2$	Complex pegmatites. Placer
Colorless, Red, Yellow, Black	10	3.5	Octahedral crystals. Four-cleavage directions	DIAMOND C	Kimberlite pipes. Placer
			B. Shows No Cleavage		
Black, Variously Colored	7 to 7.5	3.0-3.2	Slender crystals with triangular cross sections	TOURMALINE $Na(Mg,Fe,Mn,Li,Al)_3Al_6(Si_6O_{18})(BO_3)_3•(OH,F)_4$	Complex pegmatites. High-grade regional metamorphic rocks
Brown to Black	7 to 7.5	3.7	Prismatic crystals. Sometimes cross-twins in schists	STAUROLITE $(Fe,Mg)_2(Al,Fe)_9O_6(SiO_4)_4(O,OH)_2$	Medium-grade regional metamorphic rocks
Brown, Red	7.5	3.2	Square prismatic crystals.	ANDALUSITE	Low-grade regional
Green			CHIASTOLITE—where cross section—black cross	Al_2OSiO_4	metamorphic rocks
Brown, Red, Gray, Colorless	7.5	4.7	Small prismatic crystals	ZIRCON $ZrSiO_4$	Silicic and intermediate intrusive igneous rocks

HARDNESS Greater Than 7

searchable text view

A. Shows Good Cleavage

Hardness: 7 to 7.5; **Specific Gravity:** 2.6
Name / Formula: CORDIERITE / $Mg_2Al_4Si_5O_{18}$
Geologic Environment: Contact metamorphic rocks. Low-grade regional metamorphic rocks
Color: Blue, Colorless
Remarks: Embedded grains resembling quartz

Hardness: 8; **Specific Gravity:** 3.4-3.6
Name / Formula: TOPAZ / $Al_2(SiO_4)(OH,F)_2$
Geologic Environment: Complex pegmatites. Placer

Color: Colorless, Yellow, Pink, Blue, Green
Remarks: Usually in crystals

Hardness: 10; **Specific Gravity:** 3.5
Name / Formula: DIAMOND / C
Geologic Environment: Kimberlite pipes. Placer
Color: Colorless, Red, Yellow, Black
Remarks: Octahedral crystals.
Four-cleavage directions

B. Shows No Cleavage

Hardness: 7 to 7.5; **Specific Gravity:** 3.0-3.2
Name / Formula: TOURMALINE / $Na(Mg,Fe,Mn,Li,Al)_3Al_6(Si_6O_{18})$ $(BO_3)_3 \cdot (OH,F)_4$
Geologic Environment: Complex pegmatites. High-grade regional metamorphic rocks
Color: Black, Variously Colored
Remarks: Slender crystals with triangular cross sections

Hardness: 7 to 7.5; **Specific Gravity:** 3.7
Name / Formula: STAUROLITE / $(Fe,Mg)_2(Al,Fe)_9O_6(SiO_4)_4(O,OH)_2$
Geologic Environment: Medium-grade regional metamorphic rocks
Color: Brown to Black
Remarks: Prismatic crystals. Sometimes cross-twins in schists

Hardness: 7.5; **Specific Gravity:** 3.2
Name / Formula: ANDALUSITE / Al_2OSiO_4
Geologic Environment: Low grade regional metamorphic rocks
Color: Brown, Red, Green
Remarks: Square Prismatic Crystals. CHIASTOLITE—where cross section—black cross

Hardness: 7.5; **Specific Gravity:** 4.7
Name / Formula: ZIRCON / $ZrSiO_4$
Geologic Environment: Silicic and intermediate intrusive igneous rocks
Color: Brown, Red, Gray, Colorless
Remarks: Small prismatic crystals

MINERALS RELATED TO
SPECIFIC GEOLOGIC ENVIRONMENTS

Minerals Related to Ultramafic or Mafic
Intrusive Igneous Rocks

ACTINOLITE	DOLOMITE	PLATINUM	Bronzite
ANORTHITE	ENSTATITE	PYROPE	Garnierite
AUGITE	HORNBLENDE	SERPENTINE	Magnesite
CHROMITE	JADEITE	TALC	Nickeline
CHRYSOTILE	OLIVINE	UVAROVITE	Vermiculite
DIAMOND	PENTLANDITE		

Minerals Related to Ultramafic or
Mafic Extrusive Igneous Rocks

AUGITE	HORNBLENDE	PYRRHOTITE	Bronzite
ENSTATITE	MAGNETITE		

Minerals Related to Pegmatites

BERYL	Amblygonite	Euclase	Perthite
LEPIDOLITE	Apatite	Ferberite	Phlogopite
MUSCOVITE	Arfvedsonite	Fergusonite	Phonolite
ORTHOCLASE	Bertrandite	Fluorite	Purpurite
QUARTZ	Biotite	Gladolinite	Riebeckite
SPODUMENE	Brazilianite	Herderite	Samarskite
TOPAZ	Cassiterite	Heubnerite	Sillimanite
TOURMALINE	Chrysoberyl	Ilmenite	Tantalite
	Columbite	Lazulite	Thorianite
Albite	Cryolite	Microcline	Uraninite
Allanite	Dumortierite	Microlite	Vivianite
Alunite	Eosphorite	Monazite	Wavellite

Minerals Related to Silicic or Intermediate Intrusive Igneous Rocks without Quartz

BIOTITE	NEPHELENE	PYROXENE	Acmite
HORNBLENDE	ORTHOCLASE	SOCALITE	Cancrinite
LEUCITE	PLAGIOCLASE		Hauyne

Minerals Related to Silicic or Intermediate Intrusive Igneous Rocks with Quartz

BIOTITE	PYROXENE	Cassiterite	Rutile
HORNBLENDE	QUARTZ	Ilmenite	Titanite
MUSCOVITE		Monazite	Tourmaline
ORTHOCLASE	Allanite	Perthite	Zircon
PLAGIOCLASE			

Minerals Related to High Grade Regional Metamorphic Rocks

APATITE	DOLOMITE	PYROPE	Bronzite
AUGITE	ENSTATITE	PYRRHOTITE	Lazulite
BERYL	GRAPHITE	SILLIMANITE	Phenakite
CALCITE	HORNBLENDE	SPINEL	Zoisite
CORUNDUM	KYANITE	STAUROLITE	

Minerals Related to Medium Grade Regional Metamorphic Rocks

ACTINOLITE	EPIDOTE	TREMOLITE	Phlogopite
ALBITE	GROSSULAR		Pyrophyllite
ALMANDINE	JADEITE	Anthrophyllite	Riebeckite
APATITE	MICROCLINE	Cummingtonite	Sepiolite
CALCITE	MUSCOVITE	Dumortierite	Uvarovite
CLINOZOISITE	QUARTZ	Glaucophane	
DIOPSIDE	TALC	Margarite	

Minerals Related to Low Grade Regional Metamorphic Rocks

ANDALUSITE	CHLORITE	WOLLASTONITE	Clinochlore
APATITE	CHRYSOTILE		Cordierite
BRUCITE	QUARTZ		Harmotome
CALCITE	SERPENTINE		Heulandite

Minerals Related to Contact Metamorphic Rocks

ALMANDINE	MAGNETITE	Chlorite	Pectolite
ANDRADITE	MOLYBDENITE	Cordierite	Periclase
ANORTHITE	RHODONITE	Cummingtonite	Richterite
BRUCITE	SILLMANITE	Diopside	Scapolite
CALCITE	SPINEL	Dumortierite	Thorianite
CHALCOPYRITE	WOLLASTONITE	Hedenbergite	Titanite
EPIDOTE		Ilvaite	Vesuvianite
GROSSULAR		Johannsenite	(Idocrase)

Minerals Related to Cavity Fillings in Volcanic Rocks

ANALCIME	LABRADORITE	STILBITE	Laumpontite
(ANALCITE)	LEUCITE	TRIDYMITE	Pectolite
CALCITE	NATROLITE		Phillipsite
CHABAZITE	OPAL	Apophyllite	Scolecite
CHALCEDONY	PREHNITE	Babingtonite	Thomsonite
CRYSTOBALITE	QUARTZ	Datolite	
HEULANDITE	SANIDINE	Harmotome	

Minerals Related to Hot Springs

ARAGONITE	ORPIMENT	REALGAR	Epsomite
CALCITE	QUARTZ	SULPHUR	
GYPSUM			

Minerals Related to Placers or Beach Sands

BERYL	ILMENITE	TOPAZ	Columbite
CASSITERITE	MAGNETITE	ZIRCON	Euclase
GARNET	PLATINUM		Monazite
GOLD	STAUROLITE	Anatase	Tantalite

Mineral Deposits Related to Evaporite Deposits

ANHYDRITE	CELESTITE	HALITE	ULEXITE
ARAGONITE	COLEMANITE	KERNITE	
BORAX	GYPSUM	SYLVITE	Carnallite

Minerals Related to Residual Deposits

BAUXITE
KAOLINITE
MONTMORILLONITE
SEPIOLITE
Lepidocrocite

MINERALS RELATED TO
SPECIFIC METALS

IRON	COPPER		MOLYBDENUM & TUNGSTEN
Secondary Minerals			
GOETHITE HEMATITE LIMONITE	AZURITE BORNITE CHALCOCITE CHRYSOCOLLA COVELLITE CUPRITE MALACHITE NATIVE COPPER TURQUOISE	Atacamite Aurichalcite Bronchantite Chalcanthite Conichalcite Cyanotrachite Dioptase Linartite Rosasite Scorodite	
Primary Minerals			
ARSENOPYRITE ILMENITE MAGNETITE MARCASITE PYRITE PYRRHOTITE SIDERITE TENNANTITE TETRAHEDRITE	BORNITE CHALCOPYRITE ENARGITE TETRAHEDRITE		MOLYBDENITE SCHEELITE WOLFRAMITE WULFENITE
Associated Minerals			
	MOLYBDENITE PYRITE QUARTZ		PYRITE QUARTZ

LEAD	ZINC	SILVER	GOLD
Secondary Minerals			
ANGLESITE CERUSSITE CROCOITE PYROMORPHITE WULFENITE	HEMIMORPHITE SMITHSONITE	CERARGYRITE (CHLORARGYRITE) PROUSTITE PYRARGYRITE	GOLD
Primary Minerals			
GALENA	SPHALERITE	ARGENTITE NATIVE SILVER STEPHANITE SYLVANITE	CALAVERITE GOLD HESSITE
Related Minerals			
BARITE CALCITE FLUORITE SIDERITE SILVER SPHALERITE WITHERITE	GALENA	GALENA	ARSENOPYRITE QUARTZ

NICKEL	COBALT	CHROMIUM	TIN	PLATINUM
Secondary Minerals				
Annabergite	Erythrite			
Primary Minerals				
MILLERITE NICCOLITE (NICOLLINE) PENTLANDITE Chloanthite	COBALTITE Skutterudite Smaltite	CHROMITE	CASSITERITE	NATIVE PLATINUM
Related Minerals				
SERPENTINE			Stannite	

MANGANESE	MERCURY	ANTIMONY	BISMUTH
Secondary Minerals			
MANGANITE PSILOMELANE PYROLUSITE			
Primary Minerals			
	CINNABAR	STIBNITE	BISMUTHINITE

URANIUM	THORIUM	TITANIUM	ALUMINUM
Secondary Minerals			
AUTUNITE CARNOTITE TORBERNITE			BAUXITE
Primary Minerals			
URANINITE (PITCHBLENDE)	THORIANITETHORITE	RUTILE	

MAGNESIUM	ARSENIC
Secondary Minerals	
BRUCITE MAGNESITE	ORPIMENT REALGAR
Primary Minerals	
PERICLASE	ARSENOPYRITE
Related Minerals	
CALCITE DOLOMITE	

Made in the USA
Las Vegas, NV
24 May 2024

90320429R00125